Heroes of the Heartland

Heroes of the Heartland

By Jerry Cunningham

God Bless Our Heroes
Jerry Cunningham

JoNa Books
Bedford, Indiana

Copyright 2002 by Jerry Cunningham
All rights reserved. Printed in the U.S.A.

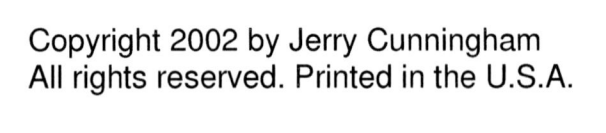

No part of this book may be reproduced or transmitted in any form or by any means, electronically or mechanically, including photocopying, recording, or any storage information and retrieval system, now known or to be invented, without express permission in writing from the publisher.

ISBN: 09706725-0-0

Library of Congress Number: 2001012345

First printing: April 2003

Heroes of the Heartland would have never happened without Brian & Linda Morgan. They planted the seed and kept it watered. To my friends and family members who encouraged me during this endeavor, thank you from the bottom of my heart. To my wife Shawn and children who gave of their time, I am grateful. My sister Sandy and her husband Ken, without you this wouldn't have been attempted, thank you, doesn't say it well enough.

HEROES OF THE HEARTLAND

When I started the numerous interviews that comprise this book I desired a better understanding of the men that sacrificed so much to deliver our freedom.

You may know men similar to these. It's possible your father or grandfather was one of those gallant men who rushed to our defense so long ago. We look at them now and see elderly men. We see them as a kindly grandfather or deacon at the church. We must always remember that at one time they were young. Their cause was noble and their hearts were as lions.

The term hero has been thrown around throughout our life times. At one time or another we have all had them. Was it an athlete or entertainer? Maybe it was your parents or big brother? As we grow older we usually cast them aside regardless of who they are.

I will not attempt to tell you who or what a hero is. That decision is up to you. I will suggest one prerequisite when making your decision. Make sure they inspire you. Be assured that when your days are long or your decisions difficult you can ask yourself, what would my hero do? If you have chosen carefully the answers may be there. After all isn't that what great people do? When the waters are rough they have the ability to pull the rest of us in their wake.

Long ago these men stood together to defend liberty. Prayers delivered some of them home; others did not. There long ago sacrifice literally affords us the freedom we know sixty years later. They fought bled and sacrificed during and after the war. Each of these men has lived exemplary lives. Gallantry and integrity are etched in their very souls. They have endured far more then most of us will ever know. Yet they haven't complained or asked for recognition. In essence the men you are about to read about once saved the world and then put it behind them.

This project has been an experience of a lifetime. In most cases the men in this book have became my friend. With them I have shared laughs and tears. I have learned a lot about these men and a little about myself.

I am not a historian nor am I an accomplished writer. I am simply a storyteller who is in awe of these men.

I started this project searching for both history and heroes, as you will see I found both.

"Freedom doesn't come cheap."
Jimmy O'Donnell
U.S.S. Indianapolis Survivor

"Lord; if you see me through this I will always serve you."
Rev. Harry Northern
82nd Airborne Division
D-Day Veteran

"Freedom Isn't Free"
Clive M. Pugh

ALTON & ALICE PUGH

BLUE STAR IN THE WINDOW

During World War II, legions of young men straight out of high school postponed their education or careers, left the comforts of home, sacrificed their well being and some even their lives. They gave up a great deal, but one thing each surrendered was their time. Can we really appreciate what this means? Three or four of the best years of these men's lives were erased for our freedoms.

These men did not sacrifice alone. They left behind parents, siblings, wives and children when they answered the call. It's safe to say that for each GI who joined the fight, a dozen hearts were left heavy until his return.

The story of Al and Alice Pugh is but one example of this sacrifice. It is the story of a young family pulled apart for one goal: the defense of freedom. Alton (Al) Pugh, one of ten children, grew up during the depression in Inver Grove, Minnesota, population 200. On March 26, 1941, Al enlisted into the U. S. Army. He was assigned to the 3rd Infantry Division based at Fort Snelling, Minnesota, after basic training.

While stationed at Snelling, Al's good friend, Kenny Crowe, invited Al to eat at a local restaurant in Hastings, Minnesota, called "Kyle's Kafe." Kenny was dating the owner's daughter. A stunning, wavy-haired brunette with piercing blue eyes named Alice Repp served Al at Kyle's. The romance started as soon as the dashing GI set eyes on this Wisconsin farm girl. The date was December 8, 1941, the day after Pearl Harbor. They had the misfortune to meet and fall in love during one of the most uncertain times in our world's history.

Al asked Alice out; she agreed. The young couple had their first date the weekend after they met. They mostly just drove around and then stopped at a restaurant, two hamburgers, no onions were ordered. Al also made time during the week to see Alice. He would go home after duty, borrow his dad's 1934 Ford, and drive 18 miles to Hastings.

It was a perfect courtship ... a memorable and innocent time for them. The two kids were head over heels for each other spending every spare minute driving around in that old car. The young waitress would sit in the middle of the seat leaning against the handsome GI. With his sleeves rolled up to his elbows, Al clutched the large steering wheel with one arm, the other around Alice. With the windows up, the old Ford crisscrossed the chilly streets of Hastings for hours on end. Conversation was light. Al had a never-ending supply of jokes, and Alice would laugh at some and roll her eyes at others. Those were the days before cellular phones, compact disc players and even car radios. The young couple had no distractions as they drove. They had only each.

The world inside the four doors of that '34 Ford was perfect. The one outside was not. The world outside was calling for Al and millions like him. Soon the young couple would be asked to give up everything.

In March Al received word that his division was shipping out to Bermuda. The task they were assigned wasn't hazardous, but it would take him away from Alice. Before leaving Al popped the question. Alice said yes. In those days young people like Al Pugh and Alice Repp felt a sense of urgency. She agreed to spend the rest of her life with a boy she had known only a short time. Even though they were young, they felt they had to live now. Many of life's riches had to be crammed into a short time for who knew what tomorrow would bring. Al and Alice were in love and they knew it.

Al's unit shipped out in the spring of 1942 and for the next six months, he stood guard in Bermuda. In early November

Al was informed that his father was dying of a mysterious infection brought on by a mosquito bite. Al was sent home on an emergency furlough to be at his father's side.

Back in Inver Grove, he and Alice had a brief respite from the war. They decided to wed while they had the chance. Arrangements were made for a simple ceremony at Al's home, flowers were gathered and invitations were sent by word of mouth. A small white cake was placed on a table so small it barely supported it. Alice wore a blue dress; Al wore his Army uniform. Al's gravely ill father watched the proceedings from his bed. Family and friends looked on as the couple made a vow to each other that would prove stronger than steel. Mrs. Alice Pugh had just taken on an immense challenge. She was now a soldier's wife while the world was at war.

There was no time for a lavish honeymoon. It seemed Al had to return to duty before the rice hit the ground. Alice found out too soon what life was like married to a soldier. In too short a time, Al was back in Bermuda standing guard. Alice wrote every day without fail. One day Al was summoned to mail call and, like always, he had a letter from Alice. This letter informed the 21-year old staff sergeant that he was soon to be a father. The letter brought him mixed feelings of joy and trepidation. His wife was having their baby, but thousands of miles separated them.

During the pregnancy, Alice stayed at her parents' farm in Reeve, Wisconsin. Her father ran a trucking business and spent most days away on business. Her oldest brother, Norman, worked the farm. Her second oldest brother, Lawrence, was finishing high school and also helped with the farm. Alice kept busy filling in with housework and farm chores. She had even taken a job making K-rations at a defense plant. Every day she wrote letters to her husband.

It was summer in Bermuda. One can only imagine the beauty: powder blue water, white sands, cool evening breezes. Regardless of this, Al would have traded an eternity in this paradise to be back home with Alice. On August 20, 1943, Alice and Al became the parents of a healthy little girl named Maureen. One month after Maureen's birth, Al's assignment in Bermuda was completed. He returned home for a reunion with Alice and his first opportunity to gaze at their baby. The new family had only 15 days together. Time was precious.

Winter came early to Minnesota and Wisconsin in 1943. By late October, the wind blew cold. It was time for Al's unit to report to duty at Fort Benning, Georgia, and then, destination unknown. Guesses were that Al's unit was headed for the Pacific campaign.

Among his few personal effects, Al packed a photo of Alice and Maureen. Then he and Alice made the two-hour drive to St. Paul, Minnesota, where Al would board a train. As the couple sat on a bench, they were joined by other GIs and their loved ones also huddled together. Soon the outbound train arrived. Nervous conversation filled the air. Hugs and tears were present as well. The order was given to go aboard. Al hugged Alice one last time and then pulled away, hoisted his duffel bag over his shoulder, and walked to the train. Alice, not knowing when or if she would see him again, watched as Al and others climbed the steps and disappeared into the train. Part of her was now empty, but she was not alone in this feeling. This scene would continue to be played out millions of times in every hamlet, town and city throughout our country during the war.

While reading of their plight, one can't help feeling pity for the young couple. A vision comes to mind of two helpless lovers tragically torn apart. This was not entirely the case. Yes, Al was gone, but for a reason as important as any. He had volunteered to be a soldier. Alice had agreed to be his wife. If the young couple had been given the choice to either hide away in Reeve or fight to defend the land they intended to raise Maureen in, they would have chosen to fight. Alice had grown up working on a farm. Al was one of ten mouths to feed during the depression. Make no mistake, these people were tough.

Al's training at Fort Benning included jungle and advanced jungle warfare. Al had always been a joke-a-minute, lighthearted kid, but when it came to soldiering, this new platoon sergeant was serious. He trained intensely and expected those under his command to do the same.

Al found an apartment in the area and planned to relocate Alice and Maureen. Two days before Alice was to leave, the phone rang. Al had learned that his unit was moving to Camp Pickett, Virginia. The planned reunion wasn't to be. Alice knew then that when she had watched Al board that train in St. Paul, it could be for the last time.

At Camp Pickett, the 77th Infantry Division absorbed Al's unit. Al would be a platoon Sergeant with the 307th Regiment K-Company. Al had a difficult time earning the acceptance of the men in K-Company. Most of the members of the 77th were New Yorkers. "If you weren't from New York or Jersey you weren't nothing." Al knew that any respect he hoped to gain from the street-smart members of his platoon would have to be earned. The 77th meshed as they trained at Camp Pickett and were soon shipped to the Pacific theater.

Back to the routine of life in Reeve, Alice helped out at home while caring for Maureen. The only change at the Repp farm was a small white flag with a blue star now hanging in the front window signaling that this was the home of a serviceman. The blue star was a badge of sacrifice. Unfortunately, more would be asked of the Repp family. Alice's brothers were drafted. By Christmas 1943 Alice found herself missing three of the most important men in her life. Challenges and dangers surely awaited the men, but the road ahead would prove equally daunting for Alice.

Not only were Al, Lawrence and Norman now gone, but Alice's kid sisters, Arlene, moved to Washington D.C. to take a job at the Pentagon. With Alice's father committed to the trucking business, the farm was in need of help. Alice had to step in and tend the 72-acre crop farm, dairy cows, and chickens. Not a part-time endeavor, this work would be from sun up to sun down for the 21-year old mother of a six-month old infant. America and the world desperately needed Al, Norman, Lawrence and others like them. What America didn't realize was that it also needed women like Alice ... women who would be asked to raise their children and keep their family farms and businesses going while their GI husbands and brothers were away protecting our freedom. Alice and others like her did it not only for families, they also did it for their country. Even though they would never carry a gun or command a tank, women like Alice Pugh were the backbone of America during the war. Our enemies found out that our men were courageous and our women were determined.

It was July 22, 1944. Men stood shoulder to shoulder in a crowded landing craft. The mist of the South Pacific Ocean blew in their faces. Palm trees could be seen waving in the bluster that morning. At any other time before or since, the men might have marveled at the island's beauty. Instead, approach to the island on that day was met with apprehension and whispered prayers. The men of the 77th were advancing on the beaches of Japanese held Guam, occupied since December 10, 1941. The U.S. Marines had cleared the beaches on July 21. The 77th Infantry was to locate and destroy the enemy. Al was the company sergeant. When entering combat it wouldn't be a general or colonel the men in the craft would follow, it would be their company sergeant. Although he was only twenty-two, Al was the father, mother and big brother to the men standing behind him. One can only imagine Al's thoughts ... were they focused on the enemy or on his family?

Fighting by the 77th was done in the jungle where the Japanese were entrenched in tunnels and caves. Dense jungle vegetation made the task even more difficult. Al's company engaged the enemy several times during their first week on

Guam, slowly keeping the forward movement to overtake the island. The 77th reached Mount Barigada using the cover of a tank to cross an open field. A Japanese sniper opened fire hitting several men including Al who was struck in the upper thigh. Within minutes the lone sniper was located and eliminated.

At the same time back in Reeve, things were pretty routine for Alice. Her days started at first light. Alone she would lead the cattle to the barn every morning and evening for milking. Fences needed up-keep and crops needed tending. After a day in Grandma's care, Alice would tuck baby Maureen into bed then retreat to her room and with weary eyes and hands, write a nightly letter to Al.

A few days after Al was wounded Alice's sister Arlene went to the theater. Before the movie started, a newsreel showed fighting on Guam. Arlene was startled to see her brother-in-law being carried off the battlefield. That evening Arlene called home to tell her mother. Not knowing Al's condition, it was decided not to tell Alice. Two weeks after he was wounded, a letter came to Alice from Al. He briefly mentioned the wound and stated he was returning to his unit. Although she rarely showed it, Alice worried. She realized the dangers and costs surrounding Al's service. Anxieties were at their highest when word spread through Reeve that one of the local boys had been killed in Europe. The young man was the husband of one of Alice's schoolmates. Like she and Al, the couple had been married only a short time when he was shipped overseas.

Al returned to his platoon. On August 10 the island was in American hands and was used as a vital air base and seaport for the remainder of the war. In October 1944, the 77th was again thrust ashore and asked to claim Leyte Island in order to liberate the Philippines. The battle was an enormous operation for both sides. The Japanese had set a trap for the American forces with four aircraft carriers. A colossal air and sea battle was fought while the 77th landed to take the island. Savage, close-range combat awaited Al and his men. While walking near a river, a Japanese position was located. Al ordered three soldiers to come with him intending to flank the position and neutralize it. However, his commander, Lt. Miller, overruled Al's attack plan and took the two men in the opposite direction across an exposed area. Al looked on helplessly as the three soldiers were ambushed and killed by a second enemy position. Al anguished over this event. Lt. Miller was also from Minnesota. On Christmas Eve, 1944, Leyte was conquered; the Japanese navy was virtually destroyed.

The Repp home contained all the trappings of the holidays: a tree, presents and a turkey dinner. Sixteen-month old Maureen was taking her first steps. Still Christmas was not complete. The three blue stars hanging in the window stood as a reminder that true joy couldn't be felt until they were taken down. By now the shinny white satin fabric on Al's star had begun to fade. It had been in the window for two years.

Weeks after Leyte had been declared a victory, small pockets of Japanese resistance remained. The task of systematically destroying these pockets was given to small squads of men. Al would lead one such squad going into the mountains to remove the last remnants of Japanese resistance. These missions proved to be physically and mentally exhausting for Al and his men. The cost in human lives was high.

On Easter Sunday, 1945, the resurrection of Christ was celebrated at the United Brethren Church in Reeve, Wisconsin. Alice was present with her family as she was every Sunday. Songs were sung and the Savior was glorified. Alice bowed her head to pray the prayer that she had repeated thousands of times over the last two years, "Lord, please watch over Al and my brothers and bring them home safely." On this same day the last battle of World War II was beginning, a battle that would claim 12,000 lives before its end.

By now the Japanese military was a mere shadow of the force that had swept through China and the Pacific in 1941. Three years of island hopping had landed America at the doorstep of the Japanese mainland. America was now facing a desperate enemy that saw surrender as a mortal sin. The most vivid example of this was the tactic of "Kamikaze" or "the divine wind" where Japanese pilots voluntarily sacrificed their lives by crash-diving their aircraft into American ships.

After the victory at Leyte, Al asked for and was granted a transfer to Regimental Intelligence. He would no longer bare the burden of leading a combat platoon. Al and his company were transported to Okinawa, considered Japanese soil, on an LST. Al and the others would find out first hand about the desperation of the Kamikaze pilots. One evening a small squadron of Japanese aircraft followed a group of Marine fighters that had been on patrol over Okinawa. Things were quiet on the LST. It was shift change for the deck hands and gunners aboard the ship. Suddenly a Japanese aircraft was spotted. Al was just below deck when he heard sounds of confusion. A Japanese plane had slammed into the ship while both shifts were on deck. Al emerged to find many dead and wounded as fire raged on board.

In Reeve Alice continued her dusk to dawn work. Maureen, 2 ½, was now walking and talking. Alice continued to write daily letters. An occasional letter, so heavily censored that she never knew his location, came from Al.

The battle for Okinawa began April 1 and ended June 1, 1945. As on other islands, the Japanese were dug in at thousands of locations throughout the island. Three months of brutal fighting, 12,000 deaths, 47,000 wounded, were required to capture the island. The price America paid for victory in the Pacific was staggering. Of the thousands of young American soldiers like Al Pugh, 55,000 had died, mirroring the many thousands of American women, who, like Alice, had been left behind to bear the sorrow of their loss.

Al received word that he had accumulated enough points to be sent home. He had earned it having fought in three of the most savage battles in the Pacific. One would think that the ride home aboard the transport ship would have been a joyous one for Al. Yet he was tormented when he saw thousands of green Marines waiting to board ships for the invasion of mainland Japan. Regardless of their skill and training, Al knew many of the men would die in that invasion. During his voyage home, word was announced that Japan had accepted surrender. For Al there was no celebrating or jumping about. He stated, "I'm just glad it's over."

Alice once again made the two-hour drive to the St. Paul train station. She wore her best dress. Al's sister, Eula, accompanied her on this joyous journey. She didn't know what to expect. Al had been away 2 ½ years. Change was inevitable in their time apart. She had taken on an immense challenge and had licked it. She had become more independent. Al had taken on an immense challenge and had licked it; surely he had changed too.

Four trains arrived and unloaded soldiers as Alice searched the faces on that muggy September day. The fifth train rolled in, again soldiers stepped from the coaches dressed in brown, and Alice wondered if she would recognize her husband. As men swirled and walked away from the train, Al's sister yelled, "There's Alton!" Alice saw him. Part of her conscience said this isn't real. The two moved closer together, all the while Alice felt as if she was in a dream. Finally, after years and worlds apart, she reached out and touched his arm. It was real; he was safely home. During their emotional reunion, Alice said a silent prayer thanking the Lord.

Photographs do not exist of their reunion; the scene is recorded only in their memories. If a photograph of Alice touching Al's weary arm had been taken, what a triumphant image it would be. Surely the photo would have captured the lines in Al's still young face and his weariness of death and killing. The photo would have captured the calluses upon Alice's hands showing she too had done her share. Yet the photograph would have been one for the ages for it would have shown that the war was over for them. They had crossed the finish line. Their reward was a free world for their daughter.

Things were unusual for Maureen when this man appeared in her home. Her life had never included this stranger. Suddenly, here he was. Al's adjustment was difficult too. Loud noises startled him. And now Alice would have a husband by her side for the first time. Within a few months Alice's prayers were answered completely when her brothers returned.

After that day at the train station they have never again left each other's side. Their union has produced four children, 13 grandchildren and 13 great grandchildren. They have celebrated nearly 60 years of marriage together. Today you will find they haven't changed much since those days riding in Herman Pugh's '34 Ford. Instead of a car, conversations are held at the kitchen table. Al still offers a joke a minute. Alice still shakes her head and rolls her eyes.

Alice was asked what made their marriage strong? She replied, "respect." True to form, Al stated he lives by the "three ma'am rule … yes, ma'am; no, ma'am; and you're right, ma'am." Al will also warn you, "If a man tells you he's the boss of his house, watch him; he'll lie to you about other stuff." Alice once again looks away rolling her eyes.

On a rainy November afternoon in 2001, Al was taken to the local fire station. Little did he know that he was the guest of honor for "Al Pugh Day," in Amo, Indiana. Al was bestowed "The Sagamore of the Wabash," by the Governor. That was not good enough for the folks in Amo, they also decided to name the new Post Office after him. True to form Al tried to joke when it was his time to speak. Probably for the first and only time Al's emotions prevented him from speaking. It seems as if everybody that lives in this tiny town turned out for the event.

They all just wanted to shake his hand and say, "Thank You." Standing at his side as always was Alice.

This question was put to Al Pugh as he sat at his kitchen table in the small town of Amo, Indiana: *What is a hero?* Al replied, "Every one who was over there." Al is correct in his belief. Every man who fought in the Pacific or Europe was a hero and I know now, they weren't alone in their bravery and sacrifice. Women like Alice were heroes too.

To Brad,
Melvin E. Biddle
C. M. H.
PFC Co "B" 517th
P.I.R.

MELVIN "BUD" BIDDLE

HERO OF THE HEARTLAND

At first glance, 77 year-old Melvin Biddle wouldn't fit today's typecast of a hero. He's not an athlete, nor has he ever appeared on MTV. Melvin lives a quiet life much like other retired men his age. Known as "Bud" by his friends and family, he enjoys golf and playing cards at the American Legion. In the spring he enjoys tending to the roses in his yard. He's a family man, married to the same gal for 55 years. Melvin and Leona Biddle raised two daughters and have been blessed with eleven grandchildren. On occasion his grandchildren come over for a backyard cookout. Steaks are the meal of choice when Grandpa does the cooking.

However, there is something that sets Melvin off from other men his age. He dedicates some of his time to signing autograph requests and gives occasional keynote addresses at ceremonial dinners. He has been the Grand Marshal of the Indianapolis 500-Mile Race. He has an open invitation to attend any future Presidential Inauguration. He has met with numerous State Governors, U. S. Senators and four U.S. Presidents who have expressed their admiration for him. Even though he left the U.S. Army nearly sixty years ago as a lowly Corporal, Generals have saluted him. Despite all of this, Melvin Biddle isn't wealthy and isn't a household name. What makes this man unique? Melvin "Bud" Biddle of Anderson, Indiana, is one of only 150 living Congressional Medal of Honor recipients and the only recipient living in Indiana. Melvin Biddle has the distinction of being one of the highest decorated Hoosiers during the World War II. Also he is a recipient of the Bronze Star, the Purple Heart and the Sagamore of the Wabash.

The Congressional Medal of Honor is the highest military decoration given to an American soldier. The medal is given to those that have displayed incredible valor in defense of our nation. Only Congress and the President of the United States can bestow the decoration. During World War II only 463 of the 17 million men and women who served were recipients, and more than half of them lost their lives during their acts of heroism. The Congressional Medal of Honor has remained free of politics and social status; sons of Presidents and sharecroppers alike have been recipients.

Seventy-four Hoosiers have been decorated with the Congressional Medal of Honor since its inception during the Civil War. Today only two of those 74 are living. They are Melvin "Bud" Biddle (World War II) and Sammy Davis (Vietnam) who resides in Illinois. Only eight men from Indiana were recipients of the Congressional Medal of Honor during World War II. Three of the eight Hoosiers were decorated posthumously, and three have died since the War.

It is rare to meet with a Congressional Medal of Honor recipient. I found that if I wished to speak with Melvin, it would require a written request to the Congressional Medal of Honor Association headquartered in South Carolina. Weeks passed after making the request with no response. One morning I received an unexpected telephone call. The magic of caller ID displayed the name *Biddle, Melvin*. Melvin agreed to meet with me and invited me to his home. I later told my wife I couldn't have been more nervous speaking to the President.

When I arrived at Melvin's home in Anderson, I was greeted with a warm handshake and a "let me take your coat." Inside Melvin's home there is little to tell you that a war hero lives there. The lone evidence is a crystal block with his name inscribed on it. The crystal is the replica presented to Melvin during the Congressional Medal of Honor Memorial Opening in

Indianapolis which sits next to a fiftieth wedding anniversary photograph of Melvin and Leona.

Melvin is much like other veterans I have met. He humbly wanted to talk about the other Congressional Medal of Honor recipients he has known. He told me stories about his long friendship with recipient Gerry Kisters of Bloomington. Kisters, recognized for his actions in Sicily, had attacked a German machine gun position despite being struck five times by enemy fire. The two had traveled to Congressional Medal of Honor reunions over the years.

While relaxing on the couch, Melvin told me of his combat experiences and the act that earned him the highest decoration our country could bestow.

Melvin Biddle was drafted in 1943. He left his job working with his father at Delco and was sent to Camp Attaberry. It was there he volunteered to be a paratrooper. At first his commanders were skeptical about Melvin making it through the physical training he must endure while at Fort Benning, Georgia. Life as a paratrooper was tough to say the least. Each candidate was pushed to physical exhaustion. Once training was completed, they were as physically conditioned as any professional athlete. Melvin had hunted with his father, Owen, while growing up making him handy with a rifle. Despite this, Melvin admits that being around gunfire bothered him in the early stages of his training. Melvin completed the grueling airborne training and was shipped overseas with the 517th Parachute Regiment. He saw combat in Italy and also took part in the invasion of southern France.

In December 1944, the Allies were poised at the German border. They had driven the German army out of France and Belgium and thought the war would be over in a matter of weeks. The 517th had even begun practicing for a victory parade they expected to have when they returned to the States.

Without warning on December 16, 1944, the German army launched a massive counter attack, which would later be known as the "Battle of the Bulge." In the fog and snow covered hills of the Belgium Ardennes Forest, the attack took the Allies by surprise. The German army intended to hammer a wedge through the unsuspecting American line in an attempt to slice the American and British armies in half and move north to capture the seaport of Antwerp. If the German plan had been successful, the war would have lasted indefinitely. As the German army moved into Belgium, it smashed through the outnumbered American defenses. Units that held their ground were quickly surrounded. The battle was fought in below-zero temperatures. Veterans of the Ardennes Offensive remember most of all the freezing temperatures.

On December 23, 1944, Melvin embarked on the two-day mission that would earn him the Congressional Medal of Honor. That day the 517th was ordered to assist American soldiers desperately holding the town of Hotton. Melvin said, "The Americans trying to hold the town were a group of cooks and clerks who picked up guns and had the guts to fight." Melvin was the company scout who would lead his unit into the surrounded town. As he moved along, he encountered three German soldiers. Melvin surprised the trio and shot two of the men; the third man ran. Melvin shot the fleeing German twice in the shoulder. Then Melvin led his unit in a close-range battle with the enemy. During the fierce fighting, Melvin was credited for locating two German tanks that were destroyed by members of the 517th.

The following day, Christmas Eve 1944, Melvin led his unit again. Melvin encountered a German soldier on guard patrol. Melvin stated, "He was a young boy about 14 years old; he had been chained to a tree. He had been chained there to keep him from deserting, I guess." Instead of firing at the boy, Melvin decided to attempt a capture. "When I approached, him he put his hands up." While stealthily moving forward, Melvin saw the outline of an approaching German patrol. "I could see 15 Germans some distance in front of me." While his unit moved behind him, Melvin engaged the enemy. The members of Melvin's unit were unable to assist, because the extreme temperatures caused some of their weapons to malfunction. Alone and armed only with an M1 rifle, Melvin fired at the enemy in an attempt to push them back. When the firing stopped, all 15 members of the German patrol were lying dead in the snow. Demoralized, other Germans in the area fled as the 517th approached.

To those who think that killing another man is something done without feeling or emotion, they are mistaken. When the forward area was secure, Melvin was asked to come and see the enemy soldiers he had killed. Melvin refused. "I'm thankful to this day I made that decision."

The Americans in Hotton were rescued due in part to one man's actions while boldly leading his regiment. It's probable that if Melvin had hesitated and not acted decisively when he encountered the enemy, some of the men in his unit would have been killed or wounded. Melvin told me that while he was in combat, he was afraid. "Fear of dying wasn't my biggest concern. My biggest fear was not carrying out my responsibilities to the unit." Fear of failure outweighed his fear of death.

On January 2nd the 517th linked up with elements of the 82nd Airborne Division and moved into the town of Saint Jacques, Belgium. Fighting continued in the snow and freezing temperatures. The fight for the city was fierce. Melvin had lost one of his closest friends Francis Bloom during the night. The Germans were firing with heavy artillery at the Americans. Melvin was lying on the ground just feet away from another American scout. As the artillery continued to rain down on them a shell hit a house near their position. Shrapnel struck Melvin in the neck causing a massive wound. The same shell killed the second American scout. Melvin, evacuated to a field hospital for treatment, was told that the shrapnel had missed his main artery by only half a centimeter.

While recovering in Paris, Melvin was asked by another wounded soldier if he knew the paratrooper who had stopped the Germans in Hotton? Melvin suspected he was talking about him. "I said no." The soldier then said he heard a rumor that the guy was being put in for the medal. This was the first indication that he was to be recognized. Without Melvin's knowledge, Capt. Roberts, the company commander, had submitted Pfc. Melvin Biddle for consideration for the Congressional Medal of Honor. When Melvin heard this, he spoke with Capt. Dean Robbins to protest. "I didn't feel I was deserving." Robbins told the protesting private, "I'm running this company; you're not." Melvin was then dismissed.

When Melvin rejoined his unit, the war was almost over. Like most GIs, Melvin was eager to go back to civilian life and put the war behind him. He returned to Anderson and his job at Delco. In July 1945, word hit the small Indiana town ...one of its own was a hero. Melvin was unaware he was to receive the Congressional Medal of Honor until he read it in the local newspaper. A telephone call from Washington following the newspaper account confirmed the news. The Army fitted Melvin with a new uniform and quickly promoted him to the rank of corporal, and arrangements were made for Melvin and his family to travel to the White House.

On August 12, 1945, Melvin Biddle along with 14 other servicemen gathered on the White House lawn. In attendance were such dignitaries as Gen. George Marshall, Gen. Omar Bradley and Adm. Chester Nimitz. President Harry S. Truman placed a powder blue ribbon holding a five-pointed star inscribed with the word *valor* around Melvin's neck. President Truman told him, "I would rather have this medal around my neck than be President." One can only imagine what this moment must have been like for the small-town boy who felt he didn't deserve such recognition.

While telling the story about his trip to Washington, one thing was clear. Nothing was more rewarding to Melvin than seeing the pride in his father's eyes. As Melvin and I looked through a photo album, he pointed out photos of his father while they were at the White House. "He doesn't look proud, does he?" Melvin stated with a laugh. Melvin was right. Even in the black and white photo taken 56 years ago, the smile on Owen Biddle's face was obviously that of a proud father. The humble factory worker was deserving of this moment; he had raised a hero.

    Since that day in 1945, Melvin Biddle has lived with an awesome responsibility. Like all other recipients, he has lived with the certified stamp of a hero. Over the years, requests for public appearances and interviews have continued. Melvin told me requests for autographed pictures come in three to four times a month. Some recipients have felt that earning the Congressional Medal of Honor was easier than living with it. Unlike other combat veterans, it proves difficult to leave the hardship of war behind. The ongoing attention is a constant reminder of an event in a young man's life where death and destruction were present. The honor Melvin has doesn't reward him with fame or wealth. Congressional Medal of Honor recipients receive a $600 monthly pension. Melvin told me that when he was invited to Florida for the second Congressional Medal of Honor Convention in 1952, he couldn't attend. "I was so broke, I couldn't go for free," he said with a laugh. Through the years, Melvin has worn his medal with grace and dignity. Melvin told me that all of the Medal of Honor recipients have one thing in common, "None of us feel like we were deserving of the medal."

Melvin has held several jobs over his lifetime. He has worked in real estate, insurance and as an investigator for the local prosecutor's office. Melvin even entered politics; he served four years on the Anderson City Council. The job he held for 26 years gave him the most satisfaction. Melvin served with the Veterans Affairs Office, a position that became available by chance. President Truman asked a fellow recipient what he was going to do after service discharge. The soldier stated he wanted to work with the VA but wasn't sure he could pass the Civil Service exam. President Truman replied, "You just did." President Truman later signed a directive stating that all recipients of our nation's highest honor can work for the Veteran's Administration. Melvin assisted veterans with home loans and disability benefits. Much like the time he spent in combat, Melvin continued to lead other soldiers.

One hundred and fifty Congressional Medal of Honor recipients live in our nation today. They are truly inspiring men. It's safe to say none of them committed their acts of heroism for attention or decorations. All found themselves in situations where they were required to put their fears aside in the face of near certain death to save another or accomplish an objective. These men should be revered, not just for heroic feats committed on battlefields long ago, but for their unwavering grace and dignity. Few if any have ever brought discredit upon the medal. Many went on to become Governors, Senators and successful businessmen. This was possible not because they were war heroes, but because they each possessed the instincts of a leader. These unique warriors are a vanishing breed. Hopefully, our nation will never require young men to shed their blood in war again thus making the Congressional Medal of Honor unnecessary.

The Medal of Honor recipients now meet twice a year. In May 1999, ninety of them were on hand to act as Grand Marshal of the Indianapolis 500-Mile Race. Shortly before the race began, the recipients were placed in convertibles and driven around the storied two and a half-mile oval. As singer Lee Greenwood sang "God Bless The U.S.A.," 400,000 spectators rose and cheered. For that brief moment in time our nation's greatest heroes were appreciated like athletes or rock stars. This was the most magnificent event I have seen in all my twenty-plus years attending the race. When I mentioned this to Melvin, he simply stated, "Wasn't that something?" Seeing the appreciation that these great men were shown told me that perhaps as a nation we do still recognize greatness when we are presented with it.

While sitting in Melvin's living room I mustered enough courage to ask him if I could see his medal. He retreated to the other room and returned with a black box. From it he pulled his medal. He then handed it to me as if he was passing a set of car keys. Melvin again exited the room to retrieve his Bronze Star and Purple Heart. While standing alone looking at the thirteen stars on the blue ribbon, I was struck with a powerful emotion. I suddenly felt unworthy to even hold such a pure symbol of greatness. For me this emotion validated the fact that only the rarest of men deserve this honor. I placed the medal on the coffee table. When Melvin returned I told him what I felt. He smiled and said that some men have served twenty years in the Military and have never seen the Medal of Honor like I just have. We all have those fleeting few incidents in our routine lives that we know we will never forget. This was such a moment for me.

I guess its human nature to search for heroes. They come in all shapes and sizes. Their accomplishments vary. They may be a celebrity or a schoolteacher. Some, however, may believe that there are no more heroes in our world. The question is open for debate. Who's to say what defines or makes a hero? Perhaps we just need someone in our day-to-day lives who inspires us. Of this I am certain, when you're searching for your hero, a good place to start is with Melvin "Bud" Biddle and the other men who wear the five-pointed star with the inscription *valor*.

Before I parted, I asked Melvin what his children and grandchildren think of him. "What do they think of their Grandfather, the hero?" Melvin shrugged his shoulders and simply replied, "They think I cook a pretty good steak."

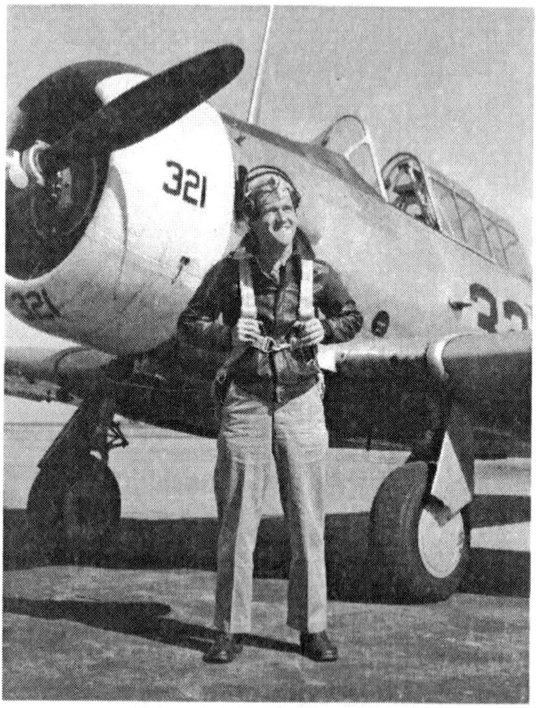
321

BILLIE HOLMES

LIFETIME OF RICHES

Billie Holmes resides in Brownsburg, Indiana, with his wife of 56 years, Wilma. The pair started dating when Billie was 15 and Wilma, 14. They are the proud parents of three and grandparents of seven. Brownsburg has been their home for 32 years and that, Billie says, almost makes him a native. Billie carries a broad smile and the enthusiasm of a game show host. Always a Hoosier, he was a star athlete at Lafayette Jeff High School and graduated from Purdue University.

Billie's entire adult life has been dedicated to serving others. He was a schoolteacher and coach, then a principal and later the superintendent of White County School System. He also stayed active in the Army Reserves retiring with the rank of colonel.

After retirement from the school system and the Army Reserves, Billie took a position as the County Veterans Officer. "I enjoyed that job a lot. I was able to help people a great deal. I would get a call from a veteran's widow. She would be upset telling me she had received a letter stating her benefits were going to stop. This was rarely the case. I would put them at ease by reading the letters and explaining what was going on." Even today Billie stays active in the community as a member of the Brownsburg Police Commission.

Service to others is a way of life for Billie. His first and greatest act of charity came 60 years ago while he was a young ROTC cadet at Purdue University. Billie had a college deferment during World War II. He might have been better served to continue his education and graduate with an engineering degree. This was unthinkable to Billie because his childhood friends were volunteering and being drafted. "I wrote the Army and said I wanted to join with my friends." His wish was granted. Billie was inducted into the Army on November 2, 1942. Billie, along with eight of his childhood buddies, volunteered for the service. The nine boys from Lafayette, Indiana, would soon fan out across the world to help defend democracy.

Although Billie Holmes is the picture of a serene grandfather today, in 1942 this was not the case. In photographs from those days, it's obvious that Billie Holmes was as dashing as anything seen on the Hollywood big screen. He literally glowed with confidence and ability. Billie volunteered and was accepted into the Army's flight program. While in Fort Worth, Texas, Billie trained and graduated as a single engine pilot.

Upon his pilot graduation, Billie was ushered to Tonopah, Nevada, to begin bomber training as a co-pilot of a B-24-J Liberator. The B-24 wasn't beautiful or easy to fly. "It was a rudder ship. It had a glide angle of one to one hundred feet. That meant that every one foot you would glide with the engines off, it would drop one hundred feet." In spite of this, the B-24 was fast and could carry a heavy bomb load. As Billie would find out later, it could also take a pounding. On his maiden flight aboard a B-24, another pilot evaluated Billie. During the flight, the check pilot asked Billie how much time he had in a B-24. Billie replied, "How long have we been up?" During the evaluation the instructor told Billie to land the plane. "I really greased her; we landed so soft, it wouldn't have cracked an egg." Billie's skills were met with disbelief from the instructor. "In fifteen minutes I had became a bomber pilot." He was assigned to a crew and continued his heavy bomber training.

In August 1944, 2nd Lt. Billie Holmes was shipped to Europe. Billie and his crew were assigned to the 330th Squadron of the 93rd Bomber Group with the mighty 8th Airforce based at Hardwick, England. Every bomber group had a chosen nickname and the 93rd was no exception operating under the designation "Ted's Flying Circus." This title was chosen in honor of its commander, Gen. Ted Timberlake.

Billie would co-pilot a B-24 known as "May-Wind-I for Item." The crew commander was 1st Lt. Hartzel C. Slider. Lt. Slider was more often called "Slippery Slider." Slider, now living in Columbus, Ohio, explains that the enlisted men on his crew had decided they needed to call him something other then Lt. Slider. "The crew had a meeting on the matter and decided I should be called 'Slippery.' Most of the time I was just called 'Slip.' I didn't mind the name one bit." Slippery and Billie trained together in Nevada. "We worked well together; we really complimented each other. I was qualified to be a crew commander but passed it up because Slippery and I wanted to stay together," Billie recalls.

"Our entire crew worked well together. You didn't have to give any orders. If Slider or I would say, 'I think those guns need cleaned,' they got to it," Billie recalls. "They were great guys from all over the country."

Billie remembers the closeness of the ten-man crew. The upper-turret gunner, Robert Poklar of Crosby, Pennsylvania, approached Billie one day. "He said his priest from back home had sent him two Saint Christopher medals. He asked me if I would wear one of them. I said sure and wore it for all 35 of our missions." Saint Christopher was up to the challenge. The medal not only protected Billie during his hazardous missions over German skies, but it also hung around the neck of Billie's son, Dick, when he enlisted in the US Marine Corps in 1974.

The crew of May-Wind flew its first mission on October 2, 1944. "We didn't know we were going up until three o'clock in the morning when they came in and woke us up. We ate breakfast about four and then met for our mission briefing at five." The formation of bombers would fly a daylight raid over Hamm, Germany. During Billie's maiden combat mission, his aircraft was repeatedly hit by anti-aircraft fire. Billie's skill and daring as a pilot would be put to the test on October 17, his fifth mission. May-Wind was hit while on a bombing run over Hanover, Germany. The plane shook violently then suddenly dropped as it was struck by anti-aircraft fire. "The sudden loss of altitude caused Slippery's ears to pop; he wasn't able to fly the plane." A frantic call was then heard over Billie's headset. Both waist gunners were badly wounded. Billie turned May-Wind for home. The most seriously wounded crewman, Doug Blankenship, was an original member of the crew who had also trained with Billie in Nevada. May-Wind lost altitude and speed after she was hit, and two of her engines had stopped. As Billie tried to keep the aircraft airborne, he could see the formation of bombers pulling away. "That's when I became scared. I knew we were going to be easy prey if the Luftwaffe spotted us." Billie and his crew were now on their own during this perilous journey for home.

Billie called out to the crew over the intercom that he didn't know if they could make it back. He announced that any member of the crew could bail out if they chose. A member of the crew asked Billie what he was going to do. Billie stated he was going to try and make it back. The crewman said, "If you're staying, so are we. Keep on pedaling." The crew aboard May-Wind had but one thing standing between death and capture. It was the skill and grace under pressure of Lt. Billie Holmes. "I found myself not only flying the ship, I was also trying to keep the crew calm as they tried to treat our wounded. My tail gunner radioed he was hit. I yelled back, 'If you're talking, you're ok. Now help the others.'"

May-Wind limped along for more than half an hour when Billie fired red flares. Red flares were a distress signal. Soon two American fighters appeared. They told me they would escort us to the North Sea, but that was as far as they could go. Once over water, Billie made a radio call to sea rescue giving their heading and speed. Finally the wounded craft arrived over Great Britain. Billie states, "Those were the sweetest words I have ever heard when it was said over the radio, 'May-Wind-I for Item, you're over land.'"

Billie had reached England, but the base at Hardwick was still 45 minutes away. Billie now faced another dilemma. An auxiliary base was nearer. By landing at that base, they would shave off thirty minutes. However, the auxiliary base had no medical personnel. For the two gravely wounded men in Billie's care, this would be a death sentence. Billie made the decision to press on. Finally, after 2 ½ hours of flight since the attack, the 2,500 x 100-foot airstrip at Hardwick could be seen awaiting the desperately wounded craft like a mother's open arms.

Shortly before landing, Billie and Slider learned that May-Wind's brakes were damaged. Slider recalls that they were going to have to stop the May-Wind with only the pressure stored in the hydraulic accumulator. Landing May-Wind would prove to be the most risky leg of this journey. Billie fought so valiantly to return his crew to base only to find that failure might come within feet of safety. "I remember praying constantly as we began our approach." The damaged landing gear was manually cranked to the down position. Seconds before touching ground, Billie cut the remaining two engines. May-Wind dropped onto the tarmac. A sudden jolt rocked the crew. The small amount of brake pressure was expelled with only one stab of the pedal. May-Wind was now in a controlled crash landing as she thundered down the runway. Billie and Slippery gripped the controls trying to maintain a straight line. May-Wind had slowed but was too quickly approaching the end of the tarmac. A hangar housing aircraft, ammunition and fuel was looming larger. "We could see people running out of both ends of the hangar as we approached," Slider recalls. Finally, the mammoth black wheels under May-Wind came to a stop within 36 inches of the hangar.

Emergency personnel quickly converged on the craft. As Billie sat among the broken controls and hanging cables, a burden left his shoulders. Despite 500 holes and two shot-out engines, he had literally willed May-Wind home. His crew was in tact and spared to live another day. For the two wounded men, they would recover but the war was over for them. In the grand scheme of things, Billie's actions were similar to thousands of prior missions flown by other pilots during the war; but to the men of May-Wind who were delivered home, this mission would be one to remember. When the crew faced their darkest hours of combat, Lt. Billie Holmes stood tall defying all odds--not for fame or recognition--but simply to save lives.

It would be safe to say that Billie was deserving of recognition for his actions. Lt. Slider submitted Billie's name to be considered for the Distinguished Flying Cross. Billie was also to be promoted to the rank of 1st Lieutenant after completing his fifth mission. This was standard practice. The morning after the mission, Billie and his crew were gathered for a debriefing with the squadron's operations officer. "This guy had never flown in combat," Billie recalls. The captain started his critique of the return trip. "He said I should have landed at the auxiliary base and not risked the flight to Hardwick. I told him I did it because I had wounded on board and they needed medical attention." Billie then spoke his mind to the captain. "Sir, I guess when we get your combat experience, we'll all know what to do." Billie stated, "He didn't like me after that." Billie's promotion was held up for 25 more missions and his consideration for the Flying Cross was denied.

Billie, along with other members of his crew, would tempt fate an astounding 30 more times over Germany. Along the way, several more close calls arose. Each mission the Traveling Circus flew was necessary to the war effort and filled with danger.

The most difficult part of flying with a squadron was that you were in danger each time you went up, and you faced the possibility of witnessing a friend perish. While enjoying the security of base, the bomber crews would spend their leisure time together playing football, card games and going on leave. Men from other crews became best friends. On several missions, Billie watched helplessly as other bomber crews were shot from the sky. "When we saw a plane going down, we would try and count parachutes. We wanted to see ten, but sometimes we would only see two or three."

On March 30, 1945, Billie and Slider flew their 35th and final mission over Wilhemshavan. Slider recalls this being the scariest mission of all. "I had heard stories of how men had flown their entire tour only to be shot down on their last mission." When it came to surviving your tour of duty on a bomber crew, so many things had to fall into place to survive. Skill was paramount. Teamwork was also important. But the thing they depended on and wanted over all others was luck. By the time the crews neared the end of their tour, they couldn't help feeling they had used up their allotted amount of luck. Billie and Slider had been dealt their fair share of luck along the way. Billie recalls a mission when they were aboard an aircraft awaiting takeoff. For some unknown reason, they were ordered out of that craft and replaced by another crew. At the end of the day, Billie learned that the B-24 they were to fly had been shot down.

The last mission went well. Billie and Slider's craft sustained only minor battle damage and had no casualties. As their aircraft neared the base traveling at an altitude of 100 feet, Slider saw a large windmill dead ahead. "I thought we were going to clip that windmill with our right wing. I turned the wing just in time to miss it," Slider says with a laugh. Billie was busy going through a pre-landing checklist and didn't notice the close call. "To this day, I don't think Billie knows about this."

After his tour was completed, Billie was transferred back to the States for training as a B-29 pilot. Billie received word after training had started that all bomber pilots not already in the Pacific Theater were eligible for discharge. Billie talked it over with Wilma and made a decision. For one of the few times in his life, Billie decided to put him and Wilma first. Billie took the discharge and returned to Purdue University to finish his education in the autumn of 1945. He had put his country in front of himself for three years. He had seen and done a lot while away from Indiana. The sacrifice made when he surrendered his education deferment was immense. Nevertheless, his service left him with a sense of pride he has carried with him his entire adult life. Like millions of others in the fall of 1945, Billie was now ready to start over.

Before Billie and many others could immerse themselves into civilian life, they had one final thing to do. It was now time to count the cost for this new and wonderful world. Billie learned that four of the eight friends he had grown up with and decided to join with would never return. Regardless of how fantastic the feeling of victory, Billie was left with a hollow feeling. On one occasion, Billie went to the home of his childhood friend, Jim Gaunt, who had been killed. He wanted to pay his respects to his fallen friend's mother. When Billie met with her, she was still grief stricken. "She stood up and said, 'Why wasn't it you instead of my boy?'" Billie quietly left the home as apologies were offered from the mother's family. As disturbing as this incident was, no apologies were needed. Billie understood. "A few years later, Mrs. Gaunt and I had that talk. We talked for hours; it was wonderful."

Billie, looking back, sums up his service as "quite an experience." Like many, he shuns the label of hero. "I have been called a hero before. I just think I was a guy trying to do a job, that's all." It's clear to see that Billie Holmes has spent his adult life helping others. His sense of duty and charity is strong. For the last 60 years, Indiana has had a man who has put others first. Billie has never been wealthy or famous yet he has made his presence known to the children in his classrooms, the veterans in need, the wounded in his care and a nation of freedom.

One of the gratifying things about living in the heartland is that people sometimes notice when you help them. Fortunately, Billie's efforts haven't gone unnoticed by his adopted hometown. Billie was named the Grand Marshal of Brownsburg's 4th of July 2001 Parade. Town folk had the opportunity to line the street and show Billie how much he is appreciated. Billie has also been named to the Lafayette Jeff High School Hall of Fame this year.

It's a certainty that Billie would have had a much different life if he wouldn't have sacrificed his engineering degree when American needed him. A man of his abilities would have fared well in the private sector. The economic rewards would surly have been substantial. It is also a certainty that knowing Billie's sense of charity his life wouldn't have been as rich. Perhaps the lesson Billie Holmes offers us is that even though he has lived a life of service and charity for others, along the way he accomplished a great deal for himself. His lifetime has been one of both adventure and benevolence. It's a certainty that when Billie looks over his life, he feels satisfied with the choices he has made. All of us should be so blessed.

Bruno Vendramin
"43"

BRUNO VENDRAMIN

INVISIBLE ENEMY

I interviewed Bruno Vendramin at his home for this book. Book interviews aren't new to him. He had been interviewed for the book *Shadows on the Horizon*. He greeted me when I arrived and I saw his wife, Ilse, sitting in the living room watching the evening news. Bruno told me he was "83 and holding." I asked Bruno what he did to stay busy. Ilse answered from the other room, "What don't we do?"

Bruno was one of four children born and raised in East Chicago, Indiana. His parents emigrated from Italy to East Chicago, a melting pot of immigrants, in 1908. "Growing up was great; us kids would eat at each others house. You had Hungarians, Polish, Czechs and Blacks living on my street."

When World War II started, Bruno was working for Amoco in East Chicago. He hadn't been drafted and his family asked him not to volunteer. In December 1942, Bruno decided enough was enough …he wanted to serve. He knew of an armed service office nearby in the city. So one day, he made the decision to walk in and join. "I didn't know who they were. I just wanted to join." Bruno had walked into the office of the United States Coast Guard. Two days after Christmas in 1942, Bruno left for training in New York. Within four weeks, he was aboard a Coast Guard cutter in the Atlantic.

Our servicemen needed food, tanks and ammunition to fight the war. These were but a few of the hundreds of supplies needed to sustain our fighting men. To transport supplies from the factory to the foxhole was a major undertaking since all war material had to be delivered to Europe and North Africa by sea.

During the first half of World War II, the German navy attempted to sever trans-Atlantic supply routes.

The Germans wrote the book on submarine tactics. They were very effective in the open sea against supply convoys. Nothing struck fear in the hearts of Allied mariners more than a stalking U-boat. Nearly 3,000 Allied ships and thousands of men met their demise crossing the Atlantic in the first three years of the War, a majority at the hands of U-boats.

Bruno was assigned to the Coast Guard Cutter Duane. "The Duane was 325 feet long, it was a wonderful ship," Bruno told me. For Bruno and others on the crew of the Duane, life on the open sea was different from anything they had ever known. "I took a shift on the watch tower one day. The guy I relieved had thrown up while he was up there. We were going back and forth, up and down on the waves. When we would go up, you felt real heavy. When you went down, you were as light as a pack of cigarettes. After I was up there awhile, I got sick and threw up too."

The men kept busy to fight boredom. "We would paint and chip paint." The crew had a simple but ironclad code of ethics. "We were one family ... you don't cheat, and you don't steal," Bruno told me. This code was important to the crew. Those members who failed to live up to it could not and would not be trusted in combat.

In April 1943, the Duane was assigned to a task force deployed to protect a convoy as it crossed the northern Atlantic to Scotland. The trans-Atlantic voyage was uneventful until April 17. The convoy had reached dangerous waters southwest of Iceland known as "Torpedo Junction" because of its heavy concentration of U-boats. The quiet morning routine was shattered as the convoy steamed east when a phantom U-boat torpedo struck an Allied ship. Bruno had just made his way through the chow line at 11:00 am. "I heard the whistle blow. I knew a U-boat had been spotted." Bruno, a loader for a 20-

millimeter gun, ran to his battle station. The crews of the Duane and her sister ship, the Cutter Spencer, sprang into action.

Anti-submarine combat in World War II was challenging. Sonar was unreliable compared to today's systems. At times crews were fighting an invisible opponent--hey knew the enemy was there but couldn't be detected. The challenge for the U-boat commander was to inflict as much damage as possible and then escape without detection.

Amazingly, the enemy sub was located inside the convoy. Depth charges were dropped from the Cutter Spencer when Sonar picked up the target. The crew of the Duane soon observed an astonishing sight ... the crew of the U-boat. "We saw heads popping up out of the water one right after the other." U-boat 175, slowly came forth from the sea. As she surfaced, tension was high among the Duane's crew. A round from the Duane's 5 inch guns were fired at the U-175. "The first round missed, but the second round scored a direct hit on the control tower." The crew of the U-175 had no choice but to surrender.

The close-range fight was suddenly transformed into a rescue at sea. Other U-boats could be out there. Bruno was one of the crew at the top of the cargo net. He repeatedly outstretched his hand as one by one, the enemy was pulled aboard the Duane. A total of 41 from the U-175 was rescued and made prisoners of war.

A crewmember painted a submarine with swastika on the side of the Duane to represent the demise of the U-175 that was responsible for sinking ten Allied ships. This custom was done much like a gunfighter carving a notch in his gun handle. "Guys were dancing the jitter bug when he finished the painting. We passed up and down the convoy so everyone could see it," Bruno recalls.

This was Bruno Vendramin's sole combat action. His right eardrum was ruptured during gunnery practice forcing his early release. Bruno was honorably discharged after this voyage. Although he served his country only a short time, the experience left him with a lifetime of pride. I asked Bruno, "Are you proud of this experience?" With a loud voice he proclaimed, "You're damn right I am! The Navy always got the credit during the War. The Coast Guard did a lot of good too."

Nov 10, 03
Harry H Northern
82nd ABN

REV. HARRY NORTHERN

RETURNED WINGS

I had the opportunity to meet Harry Northern in March 2000. In 1994 I had read a story written about him. To commemorate the 50th anniversary of D-Day Karin Johansson wrote the story. It was a true thrill to meet this man whom I had only read about. I explained to my wife it was like meeting Michael Jordan. Harry was the First World War Two veteran I interviewed for this book. The men that served in World War Two have always interested me. It's probably because that no matter how you look at it, this war was a true struggle of good vs. evil.

When we met at his Danville residence, I asked Mr. Northern to speak about his experience at Normandy with the 82nd Airborne Division. Harry was assigned to the 307th Engineers B-Company. Without hesitation this charismatic and humble man started to speak. "Just after midnight we were flying in, some of the planes in our group were being shot at," Northern explained. Northern's transport plane, a C-47 Dakota, was able to stay on course but was moving much faster and lower than planned. At that time Harry's adoring wife Betty looked me in the eye and spoke up, "Harry prayed that if the Lord see him through this, he would always serve him." In my reading of World War II combat veterans, I later found that this was pretty common--faith, training and your buddies were all you had in moments like these. As the paratroopers sat in their seats they could hear constant enemy fire. Enemy rounds were passing through the aircraft. Suddenly a red light's glow appeared in the front of the dark plane. Without hesitation the men rose to their feet. Seconds later a green light flashed. This was the moment. Harry and the others would now literally jump into the unknown. As Harry stood near the door he could see the night sky light with explosions and the streak of tracer rounds. Harry went on to explain that when he jumped from the plane, they were just above tree top level; he couldn't have been in the air but a few seconds. The exhaust from the aircraft's engines inflated his chute. Harry stated he landed backwards in a woodpile. He was shaken up; but once on the ground, his buddies pulled him to cover. Platoons were dropped miles away from their objectives. Veterans of the invasion say it was total confusion. Despite of things not going as planned the paratroopers regrouped and accomplished their objectives. If not killed by enemy fire, some of the raiders were drowned in the English Channel or in swampy marshes, just inside the French coast. These were the opening minutes of the "Great Crusade"--the liberation of occupied France. The members of the 82nd Airborne boldly entered France as liberators not as conquerors. In the black of night, this 19-year-old Washington High School graduate was one of the first allied troops to crack Hitler's Atlantic Wall. That morning the 82nd Airborne captured a key strategic stronghold, a small village called Ste-Me're-Eglise. The first American soldiers to enter battle in France were elite members of the 101st and the 82nd Airborne Divisions. These men were some of the best our country had to offer. They were highly trained and motivated individuals who had volunteered to be paratroopers, partly for the extra fifty dollars a month, but mainly to prove they were the best. In 1944 Harry Northern was a member of the most highly trained and lethal combat unit the world had ever seen. One can only imagine that would inspire young men to parachute deep into enemy held territory with no chance to escape if the amphibious invasion on the beaches of Normandy had failed hours later.

    On June 6th Harry's unit fought with the Germans. During the fighting Harry saw a wounded Paratrooper that was entangled in a fence. Harry ran from his position to remove the soldier. "I carried him back to our position." Harry then carried him a mile to a captured barn that was being used as a makeshift aid station for the wounded.

Harry Northern then told me what happened the following night. After capturing Ste-Me'ie-Eglise, the 82nd braced itself for a German counter attack. In a dense maze of trees and shrubs known as the hedgerows, the 82nd waited. Historians believe that on June 7, 1944, the 82nd Airborne's six hundred or so lightly armed troops stared down six thousand Nazi soldiers armed with tanks and artillery support. Northern, with a slight smile on his face, told me of a cigarette lighter his mother had given him. Harry went on to tell me that it was quiet and pitch black that night. "I decided I needed a cigarette and raised my lighter." "As soon as I flicked that lighter, a German machine gun opened up on me." He was struck in the leg as well as his hand. Soon Harry found himself in the same barn he had earlier carried the wounded man to. Harry Northern was evacuated back to England where he would be treated for his injuries and decorated with his first of two Purple Hearts. Out of one hundred forty men in Harry's company, one hundred were killed or wounded.

Northern speaks most proudly of the 82nd Airborne's action in "Operation Market-Garden." In September 1944, the pursuit of the retreating German army had stalled. The daring plan would be to parachute the 82nd and 101st ahead of the advancing allies into Holland to capture several crucial bridges. Northern told me, "The French Underground had plowed up fields telling the Germans that they were going to plant beets." On September 17, the 82nd was dropped into the open fields during broad daylight. Northern stated, "It was like landing on a mattress." The 82nd captured a key bridge in Nijmegan over the Whaal Channel. The German Army had already wired the bridge with explosives when Harry's unit captured it. The 82nd withstood several counter attacks defending the massive bridge.

While talking about the operation Harry's brow shifts downward and his legs begin to move. "You know that while we were fighting the British stopped. I looked over and they were all gathered together brewing tea." The members of the 82nd were shocked that while the battle for the bridge raged their British allies had taken a tea break. Over fourteen hundred members of the 82nd were killed in "Market-Garden."

While speaking to Harry Northern, it's the humorous stories he recalls most vividly. Harry told me of one occasion during the "Ardennes Campaign" when a convoy of American troops was passing a crossroad. Harry stated when the convoy passed the intersection; he could see a column of German troops and trucks heading the opposite direction. Harry just shook his head and stated, "I don't know how they didn't see us—not a shot was fired." Northern tells of another story that happened to him at the end of the war. While standing on a street corner, he could hear the roar of an approaching vehicle. When Northern turned, he could clearly see a large black convertible. Inside the car were several German officers not more than a few yards from him. Northern raised his powerful Browning automatic rifle, "But for some reason I didn't fire," explained Northern. "It was the strangest thing I ever saw; a single American Soldier was riding alongside the car on a bicycle." The Germans had just surrendered to him moments before.

Northern survived the war despite sustaining a mortar-round injury while crossing a frozen lake on a moonlit night. The 82nd had been moved in during the battle of the bulge. For this he received his second Purple Heart. Northern came home to Indianapolis and married his high school sweetheart, Betty Cooke. They had both sacrificed a great deal during the war. Harry lost his younger brother Virgil in the Pacific. Harry had Learned of his death, just days before D-Day. Betty too lost a brother; Robert was killed October 26th in France. They have since built a powerful union. After meeting Harry I have encountered him numerous times at the grocery or at a local restraint. He and Betty are never more than an arm's length apart.

While speaking with Mr. Northern, his wife Betty had retreated to the bedroom and brought out his uniform. The brown dress uniform looked as if it would still fit the retired but very active man. Betty Northern commented that when Harry returned from Europe, he had given her his silver jump wings. When she had the jacket dry-cleaned, it came back with the wings missing. Now to the novice it must be understood that Airborne Jump Wings can't be bought, borrowed or stolen; they must be earned. Harry Northern earned his wings in combat defending America and the fate of mankind. Speaking about the loss of the wings more than fifty years ago didn't seem to mean much to Harry and his wife, but it did to me. Days later I made a call to a friend, SFC Chuck Horner of the U.S. Army. Sgt. Horner was happy to assist when it came to replacing Harry's jump wings. Placing the silver wings back on the chest of this humble hero fifty-six years after he earned them was truly special to us. Sgt. Horner and I feel that this is a small way to repay a debt, not only to a true hero, but also to an entire generation of heroes.

On June 6th 2000, the 56th anniversary of the D-Day invasion and the first of this century, I asked Harry Northern to sign a book on D-Day written by Stephen Ambrose, Northern gladly agreed. Harry invited me over to sit at his dining room table to do so. The book signed by Sgt. Harry Northern is one of my most prized possessions now. I only hope that someday in the distant future the book will mean the same to my children.

By the way, if you were wondering, Sgt. Harry Northern of the U.S. Army's 82nd Airborne Division did keep that promise he made to the Lord on June 6, 1944, while flying into battle at Normandy. Harry retired a minister in the late 1989.

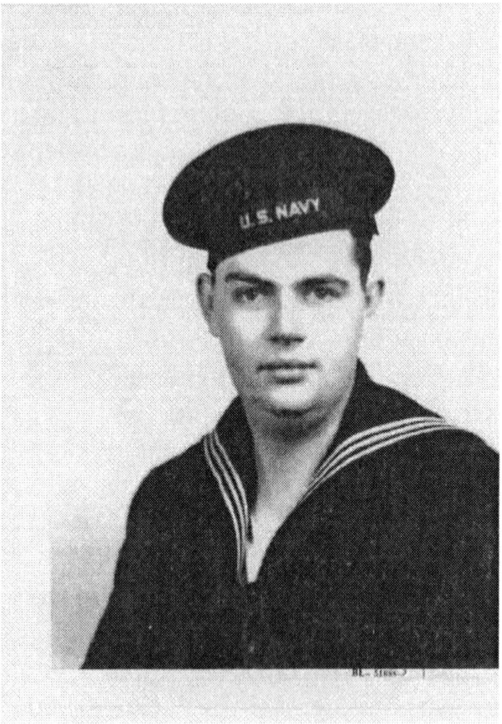
U.S. NAVY

JIMMY O'DONNELL

STILL AT SEA

Jimmy O'Donnell's story is one of service and survival. It is also a story of a man who was forced to face his painful past. Above all it is the tale of a man who wouldn't give up.

Jimmy O'Donnell was raised in Indianapolis. He attended Cathedral High School through his sophomore year. The $50-a-year tuition became too steep for his family, so he transferred to Arsenal Technical High School. After graduation he landed a job at Allison's. Then in 1944 the 23-year-old was drafted into the United States Navy. On April 27, 1944, Jimmy boarded the ship that would take him and the crew into history. She was the USS Indianapolis.

The heavy cruiser USS Indianapolis was the pride of the United States Navy. So grand was she that Admiral Raymond Spruance chose her to be the flagship of the Pacific 5th Fleet. Jimmy worked as a "Water Tender" aboard the great vessel. His job was to toil in the heat of the boiler room. Jimmy told me, "It wasn't glamorous work; but it was a job they wanted us to do, so we did it."

The USS Indianapolis had seen combat in the battles for Saipan, Tinian, Guam, Iwo Jima, and Okinawa. She had also participated in the key battles of Midway and the Philippine Sea. In all the USS Indianapolis was adorned with ten battle stars. While Jimmy was aboard, he had participated in five major campaigns.

On March 31, 1945, while engaged in the Battle of Okinawa, the USS Indianapolis was hit by a Japanese kamikaze. Jimmy recalled the plane striking the ship. "It rocked the entire ship." Damage to the ship was extensive, and nine members of the crew were killed.

The USS Indianapolis was pulled from Okinawa for repairs. On July 16, 1945, the USS Indianapolis was assigned the most secret and possibly most important mission of World War II. She was dispatched to pick up important cargo in San Francisco. Two crates were carried onto the ship and locked in the hanger deck. No one aboard the ship including the Captain knew the contents of the crates. The USS Indianapolis then set sail for the Island of Tinian. On arrival the crates were unloaded and taken to Tinian Airfield. During the mission, Jimmy worked his shifts in the boiler room. No one aboard the USS Indianapolis knew that when they docked at Tinian, a series of events were to be set in motion that would forever change the world. The USS Indianapolis had delivered the most powerful weapon mankind had ever known, the atomic bomb.

After unloading her payload, the USS Indianapolis set sail for the island of Guam and then sailed toward Leyte to participate in gunnery practice with the USS Idaho in preparation for the invasion of Japan.

On July 29, 1945, Jimmy worked his usual shift and was scheduled to return at 0400 hours the following morning. Jimmy located a place to sleep on the main deck near the aft gun turret. "It was awful hot near the boiler room. The higher up you went in the ship, the better chances you had of getting a breeze."

The USS Indianapolis, traveling alone on this journey, had reached the halfway point between the Philippines and Guam. The waters were calm that night. The men aboard the ship were either sleeping or casually manning their stations. Captain Charles McVay had received no information of enemy activity near their route of travel. Shortly before midnight, the Japanese submarine I-58 made contact with a large vessel. The submarine moved closer and raised its periscope. At 12:14 am, two Japanese torpedoes struck the unsuspecting USS

Indianapolis. The first torpedo hit the bow, and Jimmy was awakened. The second torpedo hit mid ship igniting the ammunition magazine. The enormous ship was mortally wounded. The damage caused a complete electrical failure-- lights were out and communications were rendered useless. The USS Indianapolis had no chance to call for help. Unfortunately the engines continued to run and the mighty ship maintained its speed and course. In its forward movement, the USS Indianapolis was scooping water into the damaged bow.

Despite the damage, many members of the crew were able to make it top side in the darkness when the order to abandon ship was given. Jimmy had time to reach a bag containing a kapok life jacket. Soon the ship rolled over on its starboard side. Jimmy walked his way along the side of the ship to the area of the keel. He then jumped into the oil filled water.

It is estimated that it took only 12 minutes for the USS Indianapolis to sink. It is believed that some 800 men successfully made it into the water before the sinking. The fortunate crewmembers that made it safely off the ship were floating in the pitch-black Pacific Ocean. Many of the men had time to secure life vests, but some did not. The sinking happened so quickly that few lifeboats were launched. Yes, the survivors were in a dilemma, but they had one comfort ... help was coming. If they could just stay afloat a few hours the "cavalry" would arrive.

"My eyes were burning from the oil I was in," Jimmy recalled of that first morning in the sea. As the sun brought daylight to July 30, the men were finally able to visually inspect their surroundings. They searched the horizon and the sky but saw no salvation. They were alone with no food, no water, no means of communication. Daylight also revealed that some of the survivors had disappeared during the night. Those that were badly injured or had no flotation device were the first to succumb to the harsh Pacific Ocean.

The men faced their worst nemesis the first morning in the sea. Sharks were in the area and had started to attack the defenseless men. The crew was scattered. "We were in groups of ten or fifteen. You had to stay in a group. If you didn't, the sharks would get you." The groups were miles apart at some points. As the current carried them, it also brought along the oil and gasoline that floated on the surface.

By the evening of the first day, hope of a rescue had not diminished. Surely the Navy was coming. "We were due in for gunnery practice; surely someone realized we were missing." The men had been without water or food for almost 24 hours.

On the second day, Jimmy remembers men praying out loud. "Once in a while, we would see an airplane flying overhead. It would be so high up, it couldn't see us." The sharks were still following the men. One by one, they would attack. "I could look down into the water and see the sharks swimming underneath us," Jimmy says.

By the end of day three, the elements and the sharks had exacted their toll on the survivors. Now after 72 hours, nearly half were gone. Jimmy says after so much time in the water, some of the men gave up. "They would duck their head under the water and drink the salt water. After about four hours, they were gone." Men began to hallucinate, "Hey, there's a ship over there. They would then swim away and vanish," Jimmy recalls. In other groups men would be found lifeless in their vests. Removing the life vests from the dead and passing them to the living was common. On one occasion, a sailor found that his best friend had died. He clung to his lifeless body refusing the suggestion that he remove the life vest for his own use.

Jimmy maintained his position in the group. His kapok life vest was water logged by now. "It just kept my head and shoulders above the water." Jimmy continued to pray as hour upon hour passed. Despite the circumstances, the thought of giving up was unconceivable to Jimmy. "I wasn't going to give up no matter what. I wanted to live. No matter how tight the spot, you can never give up," Jimmy says.

On August 2, the crew had been drifting helplessly for 100 hours. Hope no longer existed. About 11 o'clock in the morning, a PV-1 Ventura Bomber was in the area on routine submarine patrol. The pilot, Lt. Wilbur C. Gwinn, spotted an oil slick and circled over to take a closer look. What he saw caused an urgent radio broadcast to the American base at Peleiu: "Many men in the water." No one knew at the time who the men were and whether they were friend or foe. A Navy PBY (Sea Plane) piloted by Lt. Adrian Marks was dispatched to the area. The destroyer USS Cecil Doyle was alerted by Marks and also responded to the rescue.

The aircraft, piloted by Marks, was the first rescue craft to arrive. He circled overhead dropping rubber rafts. Against standing orders, Marks landed the PBY after seeing men attacked by sharks. For hours the crew gathered as many men as the aircraft could hold. It wasn't until Marks started the rescue that it was learned that the USS Indianapolis had been sunk four days earlier. The USS Cecil Doyle and USS Bassett arrived after dark and survivors were pulled from the sea throughout the night. The men were too weak after nearly five days in the elements to rejoice or celebrate. Some were incoherent and did not realize they were being rescued. Some drowned while attempting to swim to rescue boats.

A rescue boat from the USS Bassett located Jimmy's group. They had been in the water 108 hours. "I don't remember seeing the rescue boat; I don't remember knowing that they had finally came for us. I just remember men pulling me from the water into the boat. I knew that when they got me in the boat, I was a lot better off than where I had been."

Jimmy O'Donnell was 25 years old during this disastrous event. Jimmy, along with 317 crewmen who survived, shared one powerful and steadfast quality: they wouldn't give up. Once aboard the USS Bassett, Jimmy was placed in a bunk. "The crew members of the Bassett all volunteered to give up their bunks for us. They also had two or three guys to watch over each survivor. After lying in the bunk for a while, I decided I needed to go to the bathroom. The guys assigned to me said they would help. I said, 'No, I'm ok.' I then took two steps and hit the deck."

On August 6, 1945, the Enola Gay dropped an atomic bomb on the Japanese city of Hiroshima. The bombing of Hiroshima and a second on Nagasaki brought an end to World War II. The bombs used to force peace throughout the world had been the secret contents of the crates transported on the USS Indianapolis.

Jimmy returned to his hometown of Indianapolis in the fall of 1945. Jimmy and his wife Mary Alice planned their future. He was unable to return to his job at Allison's because of a strike. At that time Jimmy decided to take a position with the Indianapolis Fire Department. Through the years Jimmy and Mary Alice had three sons and a daughter. The future was bright for this devoted family man. Like many other World War II veterans, Jimmy refused to dwell on the past. For him and the other survivors, this was more than understandable. "I never talked about the experience after I returned home." Years passed and the O'Donnell children grew up. They knew their father had survived the USS Indianapolis disaster yet he had never spoken about it even to them.

In 1960 the crewmembers of the USS Indianapolis felt it important to have a reunion. Jimmy and Mary Alice attended. Through the years the reunions have continued. Once held every five years, they are now held every other year in the city that shares the ship's name.

Jimmy remained with the Indianapolis Fire Department until 1981. Outside of the reunions, Jimmy's willingness to speak about the USS Indianapolis was nonexistent. This all changed in 1990. Jimmy was asked to help lead the efforts to build a national monument dedicated to the USS Indianapolis.

The decision to say yes was not an easy one. Agreeing to this task would mean Jimmy would be forced to speak about and revisit the experience. "I said I would do it for one reason: it was for all of the 1,196 men." He then set off on a speaking tour in which a million dollars had to be raised. "Groups of businessmen would gather up and I would talk in front of them. At the end of the evening, they would open up their checkbooks and donate to the fund." These engagements continued for five years.

On August 2, 1995, the monument to the USS Indianapolis CA-35 was unveiled. Jimmy told me a piece of the USS Arizona was placed inside the monument. The ships were the first and last American vessels to sink during the struggle for freedom. Building the monument was not only a proud moment for Jimmy and the other crewmembers, it was also an opportunity for Jimmy to come to grips with that tragic event that happened so long ago.

Over the years, the story of USS Indianapolis has become one of the best known of World War II. I am just another in the long line of writers and historians who has attempted to tell the story. It occurred to me that surely anything I could learn had already been said. As I talked to Jimmy, he revealed to me a thought that had troubled him for some time. "We delivered the atomic bomb that killed thousands of people. I sometimes wonder if what happened to us is the price we had to pay for doing that. I know we helped save thousands of American lives because we didn't have to invade Japan. Still to this day I have men tell me they would have been in on the invasion and they thank me." After making this statement, Jimmy's words trail off in silence and contemplation.

After the monument project, Jimmy has continued his work for the memory of the USS Indianapolis. He goes out regularly to sell T-shirts and hats that bear his ship's name. The proceeds from the sales have helped pay the cost of bringing survivors to the biennial reunions. "It's been good for me doing this. It keeps me from sitting in front of this idiot box," Jimmy told me with a chuckle.

Ron Randolph, Steve Newman and I were privileged to attend a luncheon held for the survivors in August 2001. During the luncheon, I learned that efforts are continuing to clear Captain McVay's naval record. Search for the wreckage of the USS Indianapolis is also underway. I also learned that a close-knit bond exists not only among the crewmembers but also their families. The crewmembers' children played together as youngsters; now their grandchildren and great grandchildren do the same. The crewmembers' offspring have formed an association of their own named "Second Watch."

Before lunch was served, a Navy band played our National Anthem. I've sung our anthem thousands of times, but this time was more emotional for me. On this occasion, I had the unforgettable privilege to stand and sing with the crew of the USS Indianapolis. After the words, "*o'er the land of the free and the home of the brave*" ended, I watched as the elderly crewmen put back on their blue hats. In many ways, their journey is not yet complete and I began to realize why they have the slogan, "Still at Sea."

I asked Jimmy what the USS Indianapolis should mean to us now. "Freedom doesn't come cheap," was his reply. I then asked him what could be learned from those who survived? Jimmy answered with a resolute voice, "Never give up ... you can never give up."

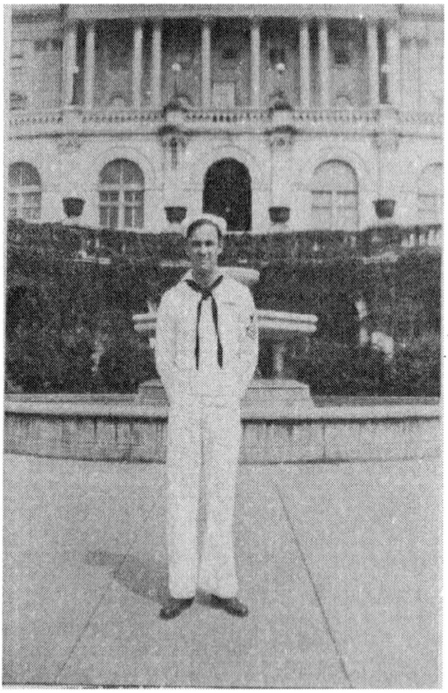

JEWEL VIDITO

THE SLIDE SHOW

In classrooms across our land, young people are taught American History. They read from textbooks, watch videos, listen to lectures from their teachers and go on occasional field trips. They learn of important dates and people. They study momentous events spanning from the Mayflower to the Cold War. Their lessons are well prepared and informative. The Brownsburg students in Mr. Nylan's 7th and 8th grade history class have been taught history much the same way with one exception. They have been privileged to learn about, arguably, the most important event of the 20th Century from a man who played a role in it.

Jewel Vidito of Brownsburg retired after 37 years of gainful employment with the Eli Lilly Corporation. His ancestors were among the first to reside in Hendricks County. He and his wife, Louise, have been married 61 years. The pair met as they were both performing at a music show in Pittsboro. The Viditos raised four children through the years. Jewel, now 81, stays busier than most men half his age. He has a handful of hobbies that includes woodcarving and genealogy. Jewel is also a talented musician. He plays the bass guitar and sings at local retirement homes. The activity Jewel finds most rewarding is being asked to speak at the local school.

Jewel has quite a set up when he arrives to share his experiences of World War II. Armed with overhead slides and music, Jewel walks the students through history he witnessed with his own eyes.

During the presentation the class is read the *Pledge of Allegiance* from the overhead. Jewel feels it's important for the kids to see the words and not just breeze through them. After all, "liberty and justice for all" was a right that he once defended with his life.

While the slide show is presented, Jewel fills the room with music. "The White Cliffs of Dover" is played. The classic World War II song is significant to Jewel. In it are the verses,

> *"There'll be blue birds over the white cliffs of Dover,*
> *Someday, just you wait and see.*
> *There'll be blue birds over the white cliffs of Dover,*
> *Someday, when the world is free."*

Jewel explains that years of German bombing had forced the blue birds to migrate away from Dover in southern England.

The class is then told about the four freedoms that were in jeopardy. "President Roosevelt once gave a speech to the American Forces in Europe; he spoke about the four freedoms. He basically told us why we were fighting. He talked about the freedom of religion, the freedom of speech, the freedom from want and the freedom from fear." Norman Rockwell featured the four freedoms in paintings for the Saturday Evening Post. The paintings are displayed during Jewel's presentation. When Jewel was not much older than the students he speaks to, the four freedoms were in grave danger. The freedom of all of mankind was in jeopardy as well. Jewel quotes the author Kurt Vonnegut when he states, "World War I was about nothing; World War II was about everything."

Jewel tells the students that an evil dictator murdered three million innocent people simply because of the religion they had chosen. He then killed twenty million Russians because he wanted their land. "He was an evil man. He had to be stopped."

The class hears about the total effort being made on the home front too. Everyone pulled together; everyone made sacrifices. Jewel's father-in-law, Edgar Hufford, lost his Brownsburg farm during the Great Depression. He, along with Jewel's wife Louise, took jobs at Allison's making aircraft engines when World War II started. Jewel's father-in-law was in his late fifties. He had both a son and a son-in-law fighting in the war. "He worked twelve hour days, seven days a week. He thought if he didn't work as hard as he could, he was letting his family and country down. Finally his heart gave out. He died of a heart attack. To me he was as much a casualty of war as the soldier was. He too gave his life for our country."

A slide is shown of the American military cemetery at Normandy, France, where 9,386 white crosses stand above the resting places of those brave men who died to assure that the four freedoms would be preserved for the very students in that classroom.

Jewel then tells his own story, which he has entitled, "*D-day a survivor story.*" In 1943 Jewel Vidito volunteered for the US Navy. His responsibilities were radio operator and twenty-millimeter gunner. Jewel was assigned to the attack troop transport ship, USS Susan B. Anthony. Captain Thomas Gray commanded the ship. "He had been in the Merchant Marines; he had worked his way up from the bottom. He was as tough as a cob, but we respected him." During his first year and a half of service, Jewel had traversed the Atlantic Ocean ten times while transporting troops and supplies. In July of 1943, he saw combat as he manned the twenty-millimeter gun during the invasion of Sicily.

On June 7, 1944, (D-Day +1) the Susan B. participated in the largest amphibious invasion ever seen. An estimated 1,000 vessels transported 170,000 Allied soldiers across the English Channel to Normandy, France. The armada was given the task of landing troops and tanks on the beaches of Normandy in an attempt to liberate occupied France. The Allied forces could not fail. The invasion of France wasn't considered a battle; it was looked upon as "The Great Crusade" ... the crusade to liberate innocent people from the control of the Nazi empire. The crusade was essentially the rescue of a continent.

On that morning, the Susan B. was loaded with 2,000 American soldiers and 300 crewmembers. The armada stretched as far as the eye could see. Despite the shear strength of force, success was not a given. On the previous day, thousands of Americans were massacred while securing Omaha Beach. Although the Allies had made headway, victory still hung in the balance. The fighting was still savage as the Susan B. steamed into harms way.

Anxieties were high for the men undertaking this noblest of causes. What would await them when they landed on the hostile shores? The enemy was determined. The German army had been preparing for this conflict for two years.

"I have been asked if I was afraid. I suppose I was. We were all together; you didn't want to be the one that showed fear. We all just concentrated on doing our job," Jewel recalls.

Jewel tells the class that about a mile and a half from Omaha Beach, a pair of earth-shattering explosions rocked the ship. The Susan B. had struck a pair of mines (floating explosives). Jewel states the explosions had thrown him into the ceiling. The explosions were followed by the dreaded sound of the general quarters alarm. As the siren sounded, confusion erupted among the soldiers waiting below deck.

"The lights went out; they were trapped in the dark after we were hit." Jewel tells of a young soldier who was below deck when the lights went out and panic started. The soldier was lying in his bunk. He knew he couldn't make his way across the crowded room to the stairs. He decided to stay put and hope for the best. Just then a bright light appeared above his head. When he looked up, he saw a sailor reaching his hand out to him. The sailor had opened a hatch above the soldier's bunk. The sailor simply stated, "Let's get you out of here soldier." The soldier later stated it was as if the hand of God was reaching for him.

A gaping hole had been ripped into the Susan B. It was soon realized the ship was sinking. Captain Gray gave the order to abandon ship. Jewel's responsibility was to report to the radio room. He was to take all top-secret communications equipment, place it in a weighted bag and throw it overboard. "We couldn't let the Germans get a hold of that stuff." Jewel carried out his responsibility and then stood by as attempts were made to off load the soldiers.

The 300 Naval personnel aboard the ship had but one objective now ... save the lives of the 2,000 soldiers aboard.

When the word went out that the ship was sinking, a Navy destroyer pulled along side. Members of the crew stretched cargo nets between the two ships. The nets were used as a lifeline for the men aboard the Susan B. Jewel recalls seeing two of his ship officers waiting to be the first to cross over to the rescue vessel. "I think they showed their true colors."

As the Susan B. took on water, a fire started in the engine room. The evacuation had gone well. Due to the crew's efforts, all of the soldiers had been evacuated from the ship. Jewel had also made his way from the radio room to the cargo net. He too was evacuated to the destroyer. The massive ship was leaning and starting to roll as it began its descent. The engine room fire was now engulfing most of the ship. Thick black smoke filled the air. Debris and oil covered the water.

The crew and soldiers looked on as the USS Susan B. Anthony's bow rose into the smoke-filled air. She then disappeared. Once the ship was below the water, a large whirlpool began to circle. "The ship we were on began to be pulled into the whirlpool. If it sucked us in, it would have pulled us under. The Skipper gave the order to give the engines full power," Jewel tells the class. The rescue ship broke away from the whirlpool.

As the rescue ship steamed away from danger, Jewel witnessed the most gallant action of the day. "I saw two men swimming as hard as they could away from the whirlpool. When I looked closer, I could see that it was Captain Gray and his Mate. True to Naval tradition, Gray was the last man off the sinking ship."

On a lazy summer afternoon, I had the honor of meeting Jewel at his home. Jewel took me through the same slide show he presents to school students. As the evening wound down I asked Jewel, "What is your definition of a hero?"

Jewel replied, "First of all, I'm no hero. A hero is a guy who does his duty. He sees a guy in trouble and does what he can to help him out. He does it without giving a thought to what might happen to himself."

I then asked, "What was the first thing that ran through your mind when you knew the ship was sinking? Was it to get these soldiers off this ship?"

"Well, yes, we had a responsibility to get all of those men off, and we did," was Jewels answer.

I then commented, "Isn't that what you just said a hero does?"

Jewel's eyes left mine; he shifted uncomfortably in his seat and reluctantly replied, "Yes, you're right."

Like many of the other service veterans I have spoken to, this man is a hero. I have often asked myself, "Is it their courage or their genuine modesty that I most admire?"

The students in Mr. Nylan's classroom leave when the lights come on and the bell rings. Perhaps they give Jewel a quick glance or a thank you as they usher past him. Do they realize what this man and many others did for them? Do they comprehend what this stranger did that still affects them today? This weekend they will share the four freedoms he defended. The little girl in the front row will attend Bethesda; her friend sitting behind her will attend Saint Malachy's. The boy in the back may voice his opinion about not wanting to get up in time for either service. Chances are they all will have food on the table when they get off the bus this afternoon. They will each go to sleep tonight without fear. Sure they take the four freedoms for granted. Nearly sixty years removed from June 6th & 7, 1944, they are still the beneficiaries of "The Great Crusade."

And yes, the blue birds did return to Dover.

John Granath

THE "DETOUR" OF

JOHN WALLACE GRANATH

A few months back, I started writing about World War II veterans for several reasons. First, the boy in me still seeks out heroes in a world where there seem to be few. Second, I feel that it's important for my children to know what sacrifices were made for our freedom. Our parents and grandparents faced an enormous test; failure would affect the fate of mankind forever. As tragic and senseless as war is, it is nevertheless an enormous opportunity for society to unite and test itself in the face of great peril.

While speaking to these veterans, I have received an unexpected benefit from their life stories. Lessons have been offered to me in bravery, teamwork, survival and strength of human spirit when faced with insurmountable obstacles. In the short time I have known these men, I have learned to alter some of my own thoughts about life. I can't help but think, if we listen carefully and put into action the lessons these great men have shared, we may become better people.

The story of John Wallace Granath is just such a life lesson. It is not simply a tale of battlefield bravery. It is an example of overcoming adversity and pushing forward when in an instant your plans and dreams are dashed.

My wife's grandmother, Mary Alice Cox, introduced me to John Granath. John agreed to talk with me but made it clear to grandma that he was no hero. I have learned never to take that statement at face value. Modesty is a common trait shared by the veterans I have met. I have yet to meet a veteran who admits he did anything out of the ordinary.

Now retired, John spends his time in activities at the Danville United Methodist Church. He is quick with a smile and handshake when greeting you. Those who know him have a commonly shared, affectionate title for him, "Gentleman."

I met with John at his spacious farm near New Winchester. John walked me to his den to retrieve some photographs. Hanging on the wall was a frame containing the Purple Heart and Bronze Star. John sat with me and told me of his life and experiences during World War II.

John grew up in the small town of Dassel, Minnesota. His Mother died when he was seven. That's when his aunts and uncles stepped in to help raise John, his sister and brother. John said, "I was raised by committee." The family was in the farming business. A simple life under the blue skies of America's heartland awaited John after graduation from Dassel High School. It was John's place to one day take over the operations and live the quiet life of a farmer.

The year was 1943. Thousands of miles away from Dassel, a war was raging. Millions of boys would be called upon to defend Europe and the world. Plans and dreams had to be put on hold. If you were healthy and of age, Uncle Sam needed you. John was drafted into the Army in June of 1943.

After basic training in Alabama, John learned that he could volunteer for pilot training in the Army Air Corps. He was tested and qualified for a College Training Detachment. John received five months of training at Northfield, Vermont. He told me he wanted to be a pilot because he had a life-long desire to fly. During his training, John was chosen to be a fighter pilot. The life of a pilot must have seemed glamorous to the midwestern boy. An officer's commission and prestige awaited him. John trained four more months. Training was in a small aircraft called a Piper Cub. Upon completion of the program, the men were given sobering news: they were all being transferred out of the Air Corps. America didn't need new pilots. The German Luftwaffa (airforce) had by this time been soundly defeated. Although the Germans were able to build aircraft, they had failed to build an effective pilot training program. By mid 1944, the Allies had total air superiority in Europe and had more than enough experienced pilots.

John was transferred to the 78th Infantry Division, 2nd Battalion, 311th Regiment, F Company. Instead of living the life of a pilot, John was assigned as a radio operator for the F Company. Unlike modern radios, the version John carried weighed 45 pounds. The radio was worn as a backpack. The 78th was sent to Europe on an 11-day ship ride. The 78th was briefly stationed in England.

On December 9, 1944, John's unit saw combat for the first time. The 78th was sent to Germany to an area known as the Hurtgen Forest. One of their objectives was to capture German soldiers for intelligence gathering. "We tried several nights in a row but were unsuccessful," John told me.

On December 30, the 78th prepared to capture a small German town named Kesternich. The 78th had suffered a bitter defeat two weeks earlier when it attempted to take the town from German control. John's regiment waited in reserve in the failed first attempt. Kesternich was located on a high area overlooking the Roer River. The Roer needed to be safely crossed to pursue Hitler's Army to Berlin. The Roer River was controlled by a series of dams, and it was essential for the 78th to capture Kesternich due to its proximity to the Schwammenauel and Urft dams. There was fear that if a river crossing were attempted, the Germans would destroy the dams thus flooding the area and stalling the Allied advance.

On this second attempt to take Kesternich, John's regiment took part in the attack. For 24 hours, the 78th was locked in house-to-house combat with rifles and hand-grenades. The Germans desperately defended every inch of the town. John's job was to relay target information from the command unit to supporting artillery. "We weren't going to let the Germans counterattack us as they had done in the first battle for the town," John told me. John radioed his unit's position while they advanced through the town. An umbrella of shells was fired in front of the Americans as they advanced. Failure to maintain communications with supporting artillery could have resulted in "friendly fire" casualties to John's unit.

At one point in the battle, John's company was to attack an enemy stronghold while a second company (E Company) of American troops was to approach from another side. John's company was able to advance behind the cover of buildings. The other company's advance was through an open field. As the E second company approached, land mines were activated. The Germans then opened fire with artillery and machine guns on the exposed troops. The men were defenseless and were being annihilated. John told me of the helpless feelings he had witnessing this massacre. For hours John stayed in constant radio contact with American artillery as it attempted to destroy the German positions.

John told me of one act of heroism that stood out during this event. A young Staff Sergeant named Jonah Kelly from West Virginia had charged two of the German positions, disabling and killing the machine gun crews. Even though seriously wounded and unable to use one of his hands, SSgt. Kelly led a small group against a third position and Kelly alone assaulted the position, disabling it before he was killed. Staff Sergeant Jonah Kelly was posthumously awarded our Nation's highest decoration, the Congressional Medal of Honor, the only such decoration given to a member of the 78th during World War II. Of the 156 members of E Company, one hundred and twenty nine of them were wounded or killed in the battle.

Written word could never describe the devastation and horror of the final battle for Kesternich…the wreckage and dead from the earlier battles lay where they had fallen…the freezing ground with gray sky above …the deafening sounds of exploding mines, shells and the constant crack of small arms fire drowned out the cries of the wounded and dying. The medics were overburdened in the deep snow and prisoners were used as litter bearers. The battle waged for two days as the buildings were cleared of the enemy one by one with rifles and hand grenades. There were many deeds of fearless determination and self sacrifice during the battle. What kept these men pressing on? John told me he dealt with combat by imagining himself as an actor on stage so that none of it was real. John told me at times morale would be low. "I remembered thinking that only three things could happen to us: we would be wounded, killed or captured."

"I prayed while we were in combat," John said. He told me of an incident when a German mortar shell (explosive) landed about five feet from him. "The shell hit and bounced; it didn't explode like it should have," John said. He knew then that his prayers were being heard.

By sunrise on February 2, 1945, Kesternich was in American hands. The 78th had no time to rest. A series of other small towns had to be captured before the dams could be controlled. John's company had to clear the remaining German positions before moving to its next objective: the town of Schmidt. While crossing the mountainous terrain, the soldiers encountered concrete bunkers known as "pillboxes." John explained their tactics for neutralizing the pillboxes. "We would open fire on the position from a distance. A 'fella' would than creep around the side with an explosive charge. We would stop firing long enough for the charge to be thrown into the opening. It was quite effective." John's battalion destroyed 23 of these positions. At one point they stealthily encircled a German mortar crew hiding in the hills. A fierce, close-range battle ensued. Members of the German mortar crew were either killed or captured when the fight had ended.

Schmidt, located six miles northeast of Kesternich, was the next objective. John's regiment traveled on foot over the snow-covered terrain. A plan had been devised for the capture of Schmidt. F Company would attack from one side of the town and E Company would circle and attack from the opposite side. On February 7, the men of the 78th were tired. Days marching had taken its toll. For 36 hours, John had been moving with the 45-pound radio on his back. "I was spent; I was like a rag," John said. The constant fighting had also taken its toll. John had lost two of his closest friends in an eight-day period.

F Company was moving along the road approaching Schmidt. John was with the command unit at the front of the line. Suddenly shots rang out from two Panzer tanks concealed in a ravine, and the men around John began to fall. The exhausted men of F Company had walked into an ambush. John remembered turning to drop to the ground for cover. "I could see the fella behind me and that's all I could recall." John and six other members of his unit were hit. John had been struck in the head and knocked unconscious. A second round had entered his hip.

When John regained consciousness, he was alone. He believes he may have been unconscious for several hours. John explained that the other men in his company, seeing him motionless, probably thought he was dead and had no choice but to retreat from the ambush. He told me he awoke and felt like he had been hit with an ax. Lying on the ground bleeding and in pain was the least of his problems. When John examined his surroundings, he saw the advance of American tanks. A fierce tank battle had erupted while John was unconscious.

John recalled passing a large crater seconds before he was hit. His only chance to survive the firefight was to pull himself to the hole. Due to his wounded hip, John could not move his legs. He removed his pack and pulled himself to the crater. Once in the crater, John felt something in his eyes. What he wiped away was his own blood. John raised his head from the cover to see an advancing American tank only 12 feet from him. "Wham, wham, wham" was how he described what happened next. Three German artillery rounds struck the American tank. John told me that the three rounds skimmed the surface of the ground so closely, dirt was thrown in his face before the rounds impacted the tank. Three of the four crewmembers jumped from the tank and ran. The pitched tank battle continued as John lay helplessly in the hole.

John told me he saw two American soldiers crawling near his position. "I took my helmet off and waved it at them so they knew I was an American." The pair made their way to John. While the tank battle raged above them, the men dressed John's wounds and gave him a shot of morphine. This brave pair weren't combat medics--just regular infantry. They realized John was severely wounded and stayed by his side until dark. In the cover of night, the men carried John into the countryside. Even though total strangers, the men traversed hills carrying their wounded comrade the entire way. John told me one of his few regrets in life was that he was never able to thank the men who saved him that day.

John was taken to an aid station. A doctor at the aid station removed John's helmet. Inside the liner was a German 7.62 round that had entered his helmet and grazed his head. John's scalp was laid open, and he suffered from a concussion. The second round had torn through his hip shattering muscle and bone. Later John was taken to Paris and then flown to England. After surgery to remove the round from his hip, John was placed in a cast from his chest down.

For his actions in combat, John Granath was decorated with the Bronze Star with Oak Leaf Clusters, Combat Infantry Badge and Purple Heart. John's battalion was also decorated with the Presidential Unit Citation for its capture of Kesternich. John's regiment received a second Presidential Unit Citation for its efforts while crossing the Ruhr River. The 311th Regiment launched a daring attack on the German defenders who attempted to repel the Allies crossing the Ruhr River.

While lying in a hospital bed, John realized that his life would never be the same. The wounds he sustained left him disabled. His left hip had massive damage to the socket; his ability to walk would be hampered for life. John's dream of returning to Dassel to run the family farm was over. He had never considered a life away from the farm. John pondered his future in that English hospital room: "The question wasn't what am I going to do, but what can I do?" Each of us has a dream or plan for our lives. Some are grand and some are as simple as working on a farm. Ask yourself, what would you do if you awoke and your dreams were gone?

John's wounds were no longer life threatening. However, months of physical pain and soul searching lay ahead. He told me that the weeks after he was wounded were low ones. While in the hospital, a Dassel High School classmate visited. Richard O'Fallon was a B-17 bomber pilot with the 8th Air Corps. John gives a great deal of credit to his friend. "He was a wonderful man. He pulled me through those tough times." Richard asked John what his plans were when he returned to Minnesota. John had none. That's when Richard suggested they both attend classes at the University of Minnesota. Richard visited John several times before John shipped back to the States.

Now a stubborn infection had set into John's hip. Arriving back in the States, he was sent by train to a hospital in Spokane, Washington, that specialized in his type of wound. John's train passed through his town of Dassel at 4:30 in the morning. "I could look out the window and see Dassel as we passed through." John was afforded only a glimpse of the home he left nearly two years earlier. He had paid dearly to defend the free world and the small town he loved so much. Like thousands of others, John was fighting a different battle now, a battle for physical recovery and the daunting question of what to do with the rest of his young life. After arriving in Spokane, John underwent a second surgery. The infection that plagued his recovery was finally controlled.

John Granath had spent a total of 16 months in the hospital. The time had come for his long awaited return to

Dassel. John told me he had known many wounded veterans who felt sorry for themselves. "Some of them began to drink." When John returned, he was armed only with the plan Richard O'Fallon had suggested. He enrolled at the University of Minnesota under the GI Bill. John studied business administration but still had no plan for life after graduation.

A surprise call came just days before graduation. John was offered a position at the Litchfield Implement Company. Peter Foss managed the store. Foss was a family friend had traveled a path similar to John's. Foss had been seriously wounded in World War I and was more than willing to help John.

While working at the farm equipment store, John and long-time friend, Seymour Peterson developed an automated system of delivering chicken eggs from the nest to the tray. During the war, Peterson was an aircraft mechanic with an engineering mind. John left the farm equipment store and, with Seymour, perfected and marketed the invention. A system of egg conveyer would enable a handful of men to run an entire farm. "The system we devised revolutionized the poultry industry."

Around this time, Seymour introduced John to a young nurse named Mary Kay Berkner. John and Mary Kay had their first date at a riverside picnic. The picnic was the first day of a love affair that lasted 46 years. After John and Mary Kay married, Mary Kay left her nursing job to care for John's aging aunts and uncles.

Through the years, the demand for John and Seymour's system grew. The pair became a formidable team. Seymour was the engineer; John was the salesman. Their device was sold in every state in the Union. In 1957 John revisited a goal that escaped him in 1944. He took flying lessons and became a licensed pilot. John crisscrossed the country marketing the system with Mary Kay navigating on some of the trips.

The system had become a huge success. John and Seymour decided to sell their company to the Anderson Box

Company. John and Mary Kay moved to Hendricks County in 1967 when John was asked to take a position with the Anderson Box Company. Even though the couple moved to Ohio briefly for business reasons, Indiana was now home. The couple returned to Indiana in 1987 to live on the breathtaking farm John today calls home. The evening I spent at John's farm I was able to observe one of the most beautiful sunsets I can recall through his kitchen windows.

In December of 1995 John lost Mary Kay after a struggle with cancer. Through the years, business was good. John and Mary Kay raised a daughter and were blessed with three grandchildren. The couple traveled extensively around the nation and world. By anyone's measure, John Wallace Granath has lived a remarkable life since he walked along that road leading to Schmidt in 1945. He admits that, after the detour, his life has been a happy and fulfilling one.

When John told Grandma Cox he wasn't a hero, he couldn't have been more mistaken. He had proven unquestionable valor in a war that saved the world. He had pulled himself through when his dreams had ended. John Granath epitomizes the word hero. His story is an inspiration for anyone who finds his or her chosen path blocked. Sometimes life leads you in an unforeseen direction. It's then that the faith you have in yourself is tested most.

The day we talked, John showed me two pieces of black lead he keeps in his dresser drawer ... the two bullets that changed the direction of his life. Thinking about it days later, I thought that perhaps for John, those two pieces of lead weren't just wartime mementos. Perhaps they were the keys that closed one door and opened another door to an extraordinary life as an innovative business pioneer and a loving family man.

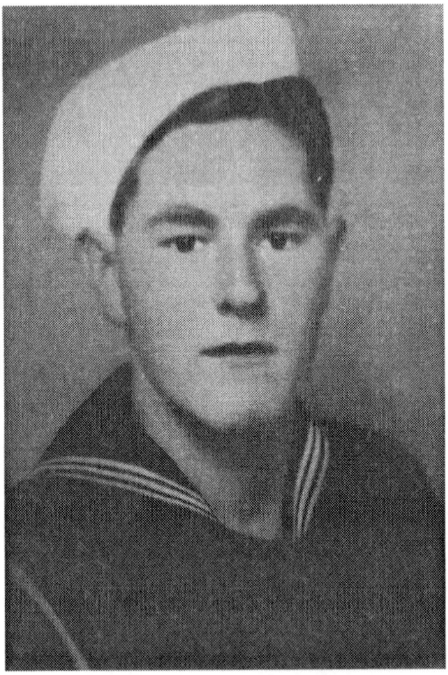

HARRY THEODORE TAYLOR

THE DAY AFTER

December 7, 2001 marked the 60th anniversary of the attack on Pearl Harbor. This was a tragic day the likes of which had never before been seen. When the Japanese military launched a sneak attack on the U. S. Naval Base in Hawaii, 2,403 Americans died. The premeditated and unprovoked assault shocked America and the world. The Earth has turned many times since that fateful day, yet the lessons learned that day are still important for America as well as for those who would oppose a free people.

Etta Eggers escaped a troubled marriage during the Great Depression. She and her four children made the journey from Nebraska to Indiana with just the clothes on their backs. After arriving in Danville, she toiled cleaning houses, doing laundry and practicing as a mid-wife.

Etta's youngest son was Harry Theodore Taylor. Ted was a dark-haired boy with both Cherokee and Irish blood flowing through his veins. He grew up in poverty. New clothes and spending money were always scarce, but love and affection wasn't. Ted attended high school in Danville. A true Hoosier, he loved basketball. He was good at it and popular because of it.

Times were simple when Ted went to high school. Teenagers then had no money or cars. A Saturday night date was a trip to the soda shop and a walk around Town Square. On a weekend night, pairs of teenagers could be seen walking back and forth under the streetlights. Instead of cruising by car, it was by foot. If things were going well for a young lady, she might have her hand held. If they were going exceptionally well for the young man, he might have a goodnight kiss or a peck on the lips. How magical those nights must have been for Ted Taylor and the other young people coming of age. When comparing those long-ago nights to the ones of today, it's understandable why it's said, "*Sometimes, more is less.*"

During his senior year, Ted decided to join the Navy. America wasn't at war. Ted probably joined to have a job and see the world. On November 4, 1937 he said his goodbyes. Hugs and kisses were shared with the family. The last hug was given to Ted's five-year-old niece, Doris. After the hug, little Doris asked for another. Ted picked her up and carried her to the back porch. He sat on a bench and sang to his little niece, "Don't sit under the apple tree with anyone else but me" and "You are my sunshine." Uncle Ted then hugged her and kissed the top of her head. Doris was picked up and set softly on her feet. Ted stepped from the porch and walked down the alley. Little Doris watched as he made his way to Cross Street and then vanished from sight.

Sixty-four years have passed since the day that Doris Watson watched her uncle walk away. "I have forgotten a lot of things in my life, but I remember those few minutes like it was yesterday," Doris tells.

On November 4, 1941 Ted had completed four years in the Navy. During that time, Ted had seen the world. He had a steady paycheck. He was even able to put his basketball skills to use; his team had won the fleet championship.

Ted celebrated his 21st birthday on November 26 while stationed at Pearl Harbor. That winter of 1941, Ted's battleship, the mighty U.S.S. Arizona, was docked at Pearl Harbor along with a majority of the Pacific fleet. On a lazy Sunday morning, numerous aircraft could be seen crossing the mountains and cities of Hawaii. Those who even stopped to look weren't alarmed. The naval base and airfield were near. Surely this was training or a drill. At 7:55 a.m. the first bombs fell on Pearl Harbor. Most of the men aboard the anchored ships were asleep or preparing for church services. Little did anyone know that a massive, well-coordinated attack was under way.

At 8:10 a.m. a single, armor-piercing bomb was dropped on the Arizona. The bomb ripped through the deck and ignited the ammunition storage room. The explosion was immense. The Arizona sank in twelve minutes taking 1,177 men to their deaths. Ted Taylor was one of them. Nothing is known of his actions during the attack. Was he asleep like many? Or had he managed to man his guns ... one of the few brave men able to put up a fight against the first wave of attackers?

America was shocked when news was broadcast of the attack. As the sun set December 7 on Pearl Harbor, fires and thick black smoke filled the air. As the sun rose again on December 8, it was shining brightly on a nation united. To be sure, the quest for revenge played a part in America's unity. What motivated us even more, however, was the fact that our way of life was in danger. Over night our nation united, mobilized and sacrificed to defend our extraordinary homeland. Following that fateful day, our enemies felt our wrath. The fight was long and costly, yet we prevailed.

Many similarities exist between December 7, 1941, and September 11, 2001. In both attacks, thousands of lives were lost. Men like Ted Taylor died doing their duty. Those who fought and died that day at Pearl Harbor can be compared to the New York City Fireman and Policeman who were rushing up the stairways of the World Trade Center as others were coming down. Our enemies then and now despise the fact that we have the freedom to choose our leaders and speak our minds. We practice our own religion and we respect those of different faiths.

The biggest parallel of all is that on September 12, 2001, the sun once again rose to find a strong and united America much as it did on December 8, 1941. Once again, those who attacked us found us not to be timid.

The U.S.S. Arizona still sits at the bottom of Pearl Harbor. She hasn't been moved nor have attempts been made to remove the 1,102 servicemen who are entombed. I have heard that each hour, one drop of oil escapes from the Arizona into the crystal blue water of the Pacific. To me the oil drops hold a message ... a statement from Gunner's Mate 2nd Class Ted Taylor and others whose final resting place is the Arizona:

"Freedom comes with a heavy price. Love America and always defend her with everything you have, just as we once did."

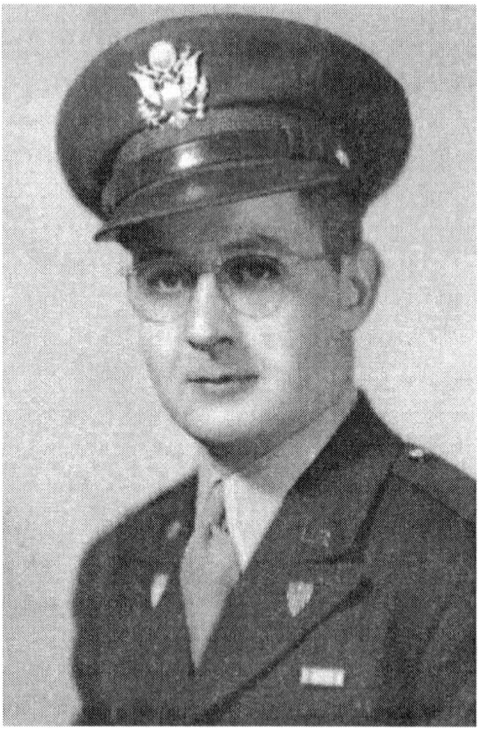

JOHN SHAW

YOUR SECRETS ARE SAFE WITH ME

During the Second World War, millions of men and women served in the armed forces. As you have read, some were combat veterans who faced death and destruction while doing their part. Many more worked behind the scenes. Their efforts were as vital to our victory as the paratrooper and bomber pilot. Final victory was achieved not because we were more determined than our enemies were. It wasn't achieved because we had developed better weapons and tactics than our adversaries. Victory was ours because of the brilliance our forces used while planning operations, maintaining supply lines and training of our soldiers.

Artillery shells were manufactured in the Midwest and then shipped thousands of miles to the European and Pacific Theaters. These shells were used against the German tanks during the Ardennes Campaign. The same German tanks were unable to re-fuel during the battle despite the fact that their fuel dumps were only two hundred miles away. Our leaders realized early that a modern war could not be won without resources. This is just an example of the superior planning that was paramount to our success.

During the war enemy codes must be intercepted and translated. Troop movements must be orchestrated across vast areas. Communications must be established and maintained between Commanders and front line soldiers. This is where John E. Shaw played his crucial role during the war.

John was born in Plainfield, Indiana in 1917. His family moved to Decatur, Illinois where he attended schools through High School. He returned to Indiana in 1937 to attend Central Normal College, where he received his degree and was drafted in the fall of 1941. John had no intentions of joining the military in those days. In the fall of forty-one, the United States Armed Services were made up of a few thousand draftees and career soldiers. Many of the regular Army or career soldiers were there only because they felt it was the best paying job they could get at the time. John reported to Ft. Benjamin Harrison, Indiana on December 1, 1941. After processing he was whipped to Camp Lee, Virginia for Basic Training as a Combat Infantry Medic. Little did he know that this was the beginning of a military career that would span twenty-six years.

History tells us that six days later an event at Pearl Harbor would change America and the World forever.

While at Camp Lee, John trained with a hundred men as a Combat Medic. When the new trainees were ready to be shipped out, he, along with a handful of others were transferred out of the unit. With only one exception, the men who remained in the unit were killed in combat in North Africa.

In 1943, John's one-year commitment as a pre-war draftee had stretched into two. John had a distinguished record and had been accepted into Officer Candidate School and commissioned a Second Lieutenant Adjutant General Department. His first duty assignment was as a member of the teaching cadre for a new WAAC Administration School in Alpine, Texas.

In late 1943, John was transferred to the Ft. Bliss, Texas Reception Center as Commander of Headquarters Company. Things were rather routine in Texas as the war was being fought thousands of miles away until John's commanding officer received urgent orders from Washington. The orders were marked 5-A, in military lingo this meant hot. They ordered Lt. John Shaw to report immediately to an East Coast staging area for shipment overseas. "To this day I don't know why I was chosen," John states. He landed in Liverpool, England in January 1944. Still the young Lieutenant didn't know what his role in the war was to be.

John found that he was to be assigned to S.H.A.E.F., the Supreme Headquarters Allied Expeditionary Force. S.H.A.E.F.

had recently been assigned a new boss, his name, Dwight D. Eisenhower. S.H.A.E.F. was the combined headquarters for the American and British operations in Europe. In the winter and spring of 1944, S.H.A.E.F. had but one task at hand, devise a plan to invade occupied France. During the next six months the destiny of the entire planet rested on the men and women at S.H.A.E.F. Only one attempt could be made. Failure would have left most of Europe in Nazi hands for years.

For John's new position he would need security clearance. His clearance was Top Secret, Most Secret and Bigot. Bigot was the Army's highest security classification. John and his fellow Staff members were responsible for the distribution and safe keeping of all highly classified documents entering or leaving the Headquarters. Now to the novice, this type of duty may seem less than glamorous. Be assured that John's responsibilities were huge. One small mistake or leak from this tiny office could cause thousands of allied lives.

Through the halls of S.H.A.E.F. headquarters, legends passed. Men like Winston Churchill, Omar Bradley, George Patton, Bernard Montgomery and Dwight D. Eisenhower toiled during those days.

"The British and Americans didn't always get along. Combined planning staffs were made up of approximately equal numbers of each country. In the early days of operations in North Africa the British would assign an officer of higher rank opposite the American officer. I've ordered the staff to get along with the job at hand or get out. The same rule applied at S.H.A.E.F."

During those days in 1944, Great Britain would be the staging area for the largest and most complex military operation the world has ever known. Millions of men from four different countries were acquiring the resources needed to throw Hitler out of France. Training, equipment placements, along with air and sea operations were all commanded by S.H.A.E.F. Thousands of written requests, responses to these requests, orders from the Combined Chiefs of Staff, The White House and No. 10 Downing Street were handled on a daily basis, around the clock. Not one letter from one page of these documents could be lost or shared with the wrong person. The AG Security Control Section handled this traffic on a daily basis without a hitch.

The code word, "OVERLORD," was assigned to the invasion plans. Not only would John and his associates be responsible for the distribution and security of the Overlord documents, they would also play a role in an immense game of deception. S.H.A.E.F. implemented an operation code named "Fortitude." "Three sets of invasion plans were circulated daily, we knew that only Overlord was legitimate," John says. The allies had sent false radio and written communications about a force being assembled known as "Scottish Command." This plan was created for the purpose of making the Germans think that the invasion of Europe would be through Norway. A second phony army was "deployed" opposite Calais, and operated under the code name FUSAG. Normal radio and paper communications were established comparable to an operation this size. All of this activity was handled at the highest security levels. This charade was carried out so that if S.H.A.E.F. communications fell into the wrong hands, Overlord would not be compromised. One complete set of plans was secured in a safe inside the small office of the Security Control Section. These plans contained both Y-Day and D-day, which made them extremely sensitive.

The events of the day ran like clockwork at S.H.A.E.F.; security was tight. Officers and enlisted personnel were limited in their access to highly classified areas. John recalls one possible breach. One evening a young Lieutenant approached John, "he said he had entered the wrong room and saw huge wall maps with the invasion laid out." The officer was quite uneasy, knowing that he should not have seen the maps. John asked the Officer, "What are you going to do about it?" The Lieutenants response, "I'm going to stay sober."

"I took my job very seriously. One morning a Colonel came to our office and identified as a General Staff officer from the War Department who had been sent to review the Overlord plans stored in our office. I informed him that I could not let him see the files unless I had written orders for the G-3, General Bull. He stormed out and a few minutes later my phone rang. It was General Bull, who informed me that Colonel could read the files in my presence. Before hanging up, he told me that the Colonel would carry his signed written order. I was concerned that I might be in hot water over the incident. Both Generals Davis and Bull congratulated me later on the way the situation was handled."

On June 6, 1944 Overlord began. The pre-dawn invasion took the Germans by surprise because of its timing and location. S.H.A.E.F. had managed to move one hundred and eighty thousand men and equipment, thousands of aircraft and a naval armada that stretched as far as the eye could see across the English Channel without the Germans suspecting a thing. Military Historians will always marvel at how a plan so mammoth could have been so successful without a single word of it being leaked to the enemy.

Overlord was not a success just because thousands of combat troops fought valiantly. It worked because of its shear brilliance and some lucky breaks here and there. On the beaches code-named Juno, Gold, Utah, and Omaha the forces of evil were out fought.

John Shaw continued to serve as the Officer in Charge AG Security Control Section at S.H.A.E.F. He never saw combat even though he volunteered for duty with a combat division. This was denied due to the knowledge of future plans he possessed.

It's an understatement to say John Shaw witnessed history up close. He had a front row seat for some of the most important moments in the war. When the Germans surrendered to Montgomery in May of 1945, the terms were hastily written on a yellow legal pad. The surrender at Rhiems was typed on legal size paper. All of these documents were processed personally by then Captain Shaw at S.H.A.E.F.

During the conflict, John Shaw and the men assigned to security control carried out their duties flawlessly. Their responsibilities may not have seemed glamorous by Hollywood standards. To the GI in the foxhole their working conditions were plush. Never the less they worked diligently twenty-four hours a day to maintain the secrecy of an army charged with the task of saving the world.

After the war John retained his commission. The one-year of service he planned in 1941 turned to twenty-six. John retired from the Reserves as a Lieutenant Colonel in 1967. John also worked as a teacher at Ben Davis High School for twenty-six years retiring in 1981.

When looking back at those days when he was teamed with the men who would save the world, John recalls the challenge they all undertook. "I was fortunate to be assigned to a headquarters that had so many brilliant men working for a common goal. All of us knew we had a big job to do. Most of us didn't know why we had been chosen."

John finds it curious that anyone would want to hear his story. "I'm sure there are more interesting ones out there." When the first member of 101st Airborne's Pathfinders touched the ground at Normandy, he came without notice. When the Twenty-ninth and First Divisions approached Omaha Beach they too appeared without warning. It happened because the staff of S.H.A.E.F. had achieved the element of surprise. Lieutenant Shaw played a vital role. It is said, the deadliest weapon is the human mind. If this is true, the collective minds of the Supreme Headquarters Allied Expeditionary Force were the deadliest of all.

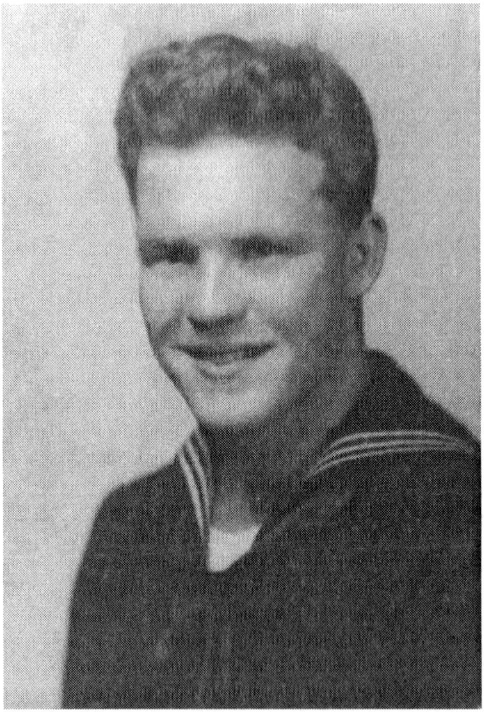

JOHN KNOX

THE TESTED

There comes a time in almost every person's life when they are tested. I'm not referring to the pre-marriage blood test or the SAT. It's the test that forms the opinion you have of yourself--the test that shows no one other than you what's inside. Many of us have taken such tests. Thousands of examples are out there ... a person who decides to climb a mountain ...the mother who decides to run a marathon ...the student who decides to go back and finish a degree. These people are all tested. The test that matters most isn't given to you; it's the one you choose to take yourself. It's that time in life when you decide to call out every ounce of physical or mental strength you can muster. When your test is passed, it serves you for the rest of your life. The satisfaction of one day looking at yourself in the mirror and saying, "I did it!" is the only reward for such self-imposed challenges.

John Knox is a man who knows what the test means. For a relatively short time in his early life, he took a challenge that would lead him around the world. Each step of the way, his endurance and commitment were put to the test. The results have remained with him the rest of his life.

In 1943 the world was at war. Red-headed John Knox was finishing his senior year playing football and baseball and boxing golden gloves at Howe High School on the Indianapolis east side. Like most in the class of '43, John was eager to join the fight. He felt it was an embarrassment not to team up with Uncle Sam to do his part. He was energetic and ready.

Before graduation, John began testing for entrance into the Navy's Flight School. John passed the exams and awaited orders; but even after John finished school, the orders hadn't come. Months went by with no response from the Navy. John was anxious despite several assurances from the Navy that his training would start soon.

In July many of John's former schoolmates returned from basic training. John was embarrassed, and his patience had been exhausted. John, only 17, had to convince his father to sign a waiver enabling him to enlist. His father agreed. John had chosen the Navy Construction Battalion (CBs) for his assignment. In October 1943, John was stationed at Camp Peary, Virginia, for basic training. John did well in his training and looked forward to his assignment. Near the end of basic training, the "green" recruits were gathered to meet with two sailors.

"The two guys were the biggest, baddest fellas I had ever seen," John recalled.

The duo had come to inform the recruits of a top-secret, specialized unit called Naval Combat Demolition Unit (NCDU). The program, made up of volunteers, was still in its infancy. The Navy realized it needed personnel who were trained to work with explosives. The NCDUs were to lead the way on amphibious invasions. They would clear man-made obstacles that would impede landing craft and tanks from the sea from advancing on enemy held positions.

"They really made a bloody deal out of it," John recalled.

The recruits were told up front that to be considered for the NCDU, they must be 22 and have construction experience. One of the sailors stated as the presentation ended, "We're not trying to recruit you; we're just telling you about the program."

The adventurous life of an NCDU member was alluring to John. As soon as the presentation ended, John approached the sailors. "I would like to join," John told the men. He was then asked how old he was. John had just turned 18. The pair stated he was too young for the unit. John replied, "I know, but I still want to join." John was then asked if he was an athlete in high school. He was. The men then asked what his interests were. For some unknown reason, John told the men he liked to work on outboard motors. "I can tear 'em apart and put 'em back together." This somewhat innocent hobby caught the attention of the two men. John was told to stay in the room as the pair exited to talk. They returned and told John he would be given a chance. He was told by one of the men, "I'm warning you, we're going to try and run you off." John replied, "If you think you can do it, do it." To this day John blames that arrogant response on his red hair.

John was assigned to the third NCDU class. Four grueling weeks lay ahead. Distance running, overhead presses with a rifle, obstacle course running and carrying a 400-pound log were all part of the physical training. The men also were given their first exposure to explosives training. They trained with shaped charges, TNT as well as composition C. Men were dropping out of the class. "Every night when I went back to the barracks I would see two or three more empty bunks." When the four-week course ended, John was one of the 30 candidates remaining of the original 120.

These 30 were then sent to Fort Pierce, Florida, for an extensive six-weeks of additional training. Fort Pierce was a desolate place. The area was infested with snakes, alligators and sand fleas. The men trained in the heat and humidity of summer. It was there they were introduced to water training. When not in explosives training, the men would swim. They were expected to swim two miles. As the training progressed, the physical and psychological demands increased. At times the men were subjected to crawling through swampy marshes while live ammunition was fired above their heads.

John thought about quitting every day. There would have been no shame in walking away. He could return to the CBs and play an important role with that unit. No one would have blamed the kid for giving up, but John refused. "Every night I would lye in my bunk and agonize about quitting. I know if I would have left I would have felt like a failure. I'm sure it would have stayed with me the rest of my life." Several things kept him going. Pride, along with his deep desire to become a member of the unit, played its part. What mostly carried him was the intense belief that neither the instructors nor the course could beat him.

The final week of class called "hell week" pushed the candidates to physical exhaustion. The tradition started then remains today with NCDU's successors, the Navy Seals. During "hell week" only two hours of sleep a night was allowed. Groups of men were given simulated missions called *problems* to complete. "They would drop us off in the swamp and tell us to find our way back by morning or we would have to do it again." John sums up "hell week" in one word, "inhuman." John completed the training. His class had been formed into highly skilled members of the Navy's most elite force--U.S. Navy Combat Demolition Units.

John was sent on a short leave home to Indianapolis. The unit was cloaked in secrecy and their whereabouts was top secret. Without divulging his unit to his parents, John devised a plan to let them know where he was in the world. John and his parents bought matching almanacs. John would write a letter home and mention a page number. His parents knew to look at the almanac to know his location. This would have been frowned upon by NCDU command, but John felt it was the least he could do for his worried parents.

In early 1944, John was shipped to the European theater. He was teamed with five other men that formed his unit--a grab bag of American backgrounds. Unit 50 consisted of a half-blooded American Indian from Montana, a man of Polish descent, a commander from New England, and one that John referred to as a "hillbilly." Still only eighteen years old, John was nicknamed "the baby."

Unit 50 was stationed in Salerno, Italy. Their days consisted of training and an occasional demolition of a wrecked ship in Naples harbor. In late May 1944, his unit heard rumors that the invasion of France would occur soon. John's unit was told they might be flown to England to lead the invasion. This was not to be. On June 6, 1944, the Allies invaded France at Normandy. The Navy Combat Demolition Units boldly led the massive pre-dawn invasion. Despite high causalities, the

NCDU's performance was invaluable. John's unit did not take part in the D-Day invasion.

By mid August 1944, the Allies had established a foothold in France. On August 15 a second invasion was launched in southern France. This time Unit 50 played a key role. A small town named Saint Raphael sat along the coast. The beaches were blocked with numerous steel and concrete barriers. The barriers were in place to stop landing crafts from unloading. John's six-man unit was assigned the task of creating a diversion. They would destroy the obstacles at Saint Raphael causing the Germans to redeploy their defenses while the main invasion force would land to the north. Just after dawn, John's unit approached the beach in a small rubber raft. Five men exited the boat and placed explosives on the obstacles. The Germans defending the beach began firing at the men. Despite constant fire, John's unit methodically continued their mission. When the explosives were in place, the men swam back to the boat and pulled away. Minutes later the explosives detonated. Sand, concrete and steel were blown hundreds of feet in the air. What happened next is still a subject of disbelief for John. "The Germans that were firing at us came pouring out of their bunkers with their hands up. They thought we were bombing them and chose to surrender." The dilemma Unit 50 had then was what to do with the Germans? John's commander told John and another man to swim ashore to take them prisoner. One major problem existed; the Americans were unarmed. Despite this fact, John followed orders and went in. "There I was with 27 enemy soldiers standing in front of me. The only weapon I had was a knife. It was a pretty tense couple of minutes." Soon troops from the invasion force arrived to take the prisoners.

Three weeks after the invasion, John's unit was shipped back to the States for redeployment. John was given the choice of taking an assignment as an instructor or transfer to the Pacific theater to fight the Japanese. Johns red hair betrayed him again; he requested the combat assignment in the Pacific.

John was given a 30-day leave to return home. Before taking leave, the NCDU members were warned about divulging their unit's activities. "They threatened to hang us if we told a soul." While on leave John didn't speak about his top-secret unit except with his father. John was safe in telling his father; he didn't believe a word of it. "My dad was a WWI veteran; he told me I was full of it."

When his leave was over, John boarded a troop train destined for San Diego. "Something that has stood out in my mind was when we would stop in small towns along the way, local woman would greet us with cakes, brownies and other food. This made an effect on us." Unlike other combat veterans of that time, John had the unique privilege of seeing how much his service meant to the people he was defending.

In the fall of 1944, John Knox was shipped to the island of Maui. The U.S. had been fighting a costly battle in the Pacific against the Japanese since the surprise attack on Pearl Harbor in December 1941. Many amphibious invasions had taken place. It was believed that the NCDU could play an important role. Larger teams of men called Underwater Demolition Teams (UDT) replaced the six-man units used in Europe.

Even though training was tough, John maintained a sense of humor. On one occasion an Admiral came in to observe a nighttime exercise. The Teams were experimenting with silver hoods they would wear over their heads. The hoods were designed to hide them in the surf. While John and his swim partner neared the shore they saw a native Islander fishing while drinking from a bottle of rum. John couldn't resist. The men swam within a few feet of the Islander. They then pulled the fishing line. When the man looked into the water to investigate, John and his partner jumped into the air screaming as loud as they could. "That guy was scared to death. He dropped his pole and ran off. He left a stringer full of fish and his bottle of rum." Due to John's prank the exercise was ruined. Thankfully the Admiral had a sense of humor; John's commander did not. He was furious at us. We were restricted to base for two weeks after that but it was worth it.

In late March 1945, John's team was sent to the Ie Shima Islands located near Iwo Jima. The islands were marked for an Allied invasion. UDT would go in first. They were given the task of locating coral reefs that could ground American ships. They also were to locate and report enemy positions to the Marines. Shortly after John and his team were in the water, Japanese defenders opened fire with artillery. Shells were exploding in the water as the team gathered their information. A shell hit close to a team officer rendering him unconscious. John swam to him, inflated his emergency vest and pulled the wounded officer with him as he completed the mission. John then swam through enemy fire pulling the officer to a rescue boat.

While UDT was stationed on the beaches of Ie Shima sobering news came in. Beloved War Correspondent and Hoosier Ernie Pyle had been killed. "Some of us cried, he was our hero."

After Iwo Jima and Okinawa fell, the Japanese military fought a losing war. John and other members of the Navy's UDT had constantly trained while in the Pacific. The men were unsure what their objective was. Unknown to John at the time was that they were being prepared for the mainland invasion of Japan with UDT leading the way. The invasion force would dwarf that used during the invasion of France. The Japanese people were prepared to die in defense of their soil. Every man woman and child would await the Americans when they set foot on the beaches of Japan. Casualties would be staggering; death awaited thousand of Americans when the final battle of the war was initiated.

On August 6, 1945, President Harry S. Truman gave the order to drop the first of two atomic bombs on Japan. An estimated 140,000 Japanese were killed in the bombings before the Japanese willingness to wage war was over. "Over the years, I have heard people say that we shouldn't have used nuclear bombs on Japan. I disagree. I know in my heart thousands of Americans are alive because we dropped those bombs."

On September 2, the surrender document was signed on the deck of the USS Missouri anchored in Tokyo harbor. With the stroke of a pen, the six-year WWII ended. While the documents were being signed, John and his team were stationed in the harbor. They were on hand to locate any explosives that may have been placed by saboteurs.

The horror of war wasn't over for the UDT. They were sent to the island of Hokkaido, north of mainland Japan. The 80-man team would be the occupying force for a city of Hokodate population 100,000. Their first objective was to liberate a prisoner-of-war camp located near the city. The British and Australian soldiers, enduring years of mistreatment, looked like skeletons--some weighed less than 100 pounds when rescued. John sums up what they found at the camp as "nightmare stuff."

John returned home in the fall of 1945. Weeks later a reporter from an Indianapolis Times interviewed him. An article later appeared in the paper telling of the top-secret Navy Underwater Demolition Team. John's father then believed the stories his son had told him.

John attended college at Canterbury College. He studied education and planned a teaching career. While in school, he met a young girl named Norma Turcotte. The pair married in 1949. John and Norma raised four children. John decided against teaching and joined the family business as an electrician. Norma worked with the mentally handicapped at Opportunity Cottage. The center is a facility where handicapped adults are trained in job skills. While Norma was the Executive Director she helped plan and develop the present day Sycamore Center. The couple lives quietly in a home built in 1890. It sits perched atop a hill overlooking Danville.

John Knox's sense of humor remains as sharp as ever. While interviewing him he requested that his rather handsome looks and marvelous physic be mentioned.

He still plays an active role with the Navy S.E.A.L.S. The Navy has asked him to be the contact person for any young man who wishes to one day follow in his footsteps. If a young man from Indiana decides he wants to be a candidate for the SEAL Teams he is given John's number. He will then be told what to expect.

The UDT/SEAL community is one of both pride and tradition. Men like John Knox are looked upon as father figures. They were the first; they set the bar.

Not so long ago our world passed through desperate times. Fortunately men like John were coming of age. Most weren't drafted; they couldn' t wait to put up a fight. "We were pretty patriotic before we joined the service. We were even more patriotic when the war was over." Millions of men and woman mustered everything they had inside of them to create the mechanism that would liberate the world and defend democracy. Millions of young men just like John challenged themselves to become the best they could be at a time when we needed it most. John, along with many others, chose to be in harm's way during the crisis. Half a million of these men died for that decision. A motto inscribed on a grave marker at Arlington National Cemetery perhaps sums up best what courageous men like John believe: "It is better to have lived one day as a lion then one thousand as a lamb."

You can rarely coax John into telling about his experiences. When he does talk of his experiences, an unmistakable look of satisfaction envelops John's face. His hair is no longer red and time has weathered his face; but if you look closely, you will see the unmistakable eyes of a warrior.

His children have asked him to record his experiences, put them on paper or make an audio recording. John never has. One would wonder why a man who experienced so much would be reluctant to talk about it. It possibly boils down to the fact that John Knox passed "the test" long ago and hasn't had to prove anything to anyone since, especially to himself.

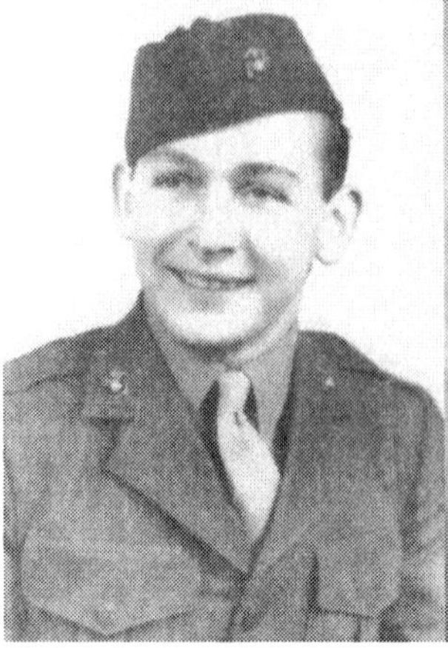

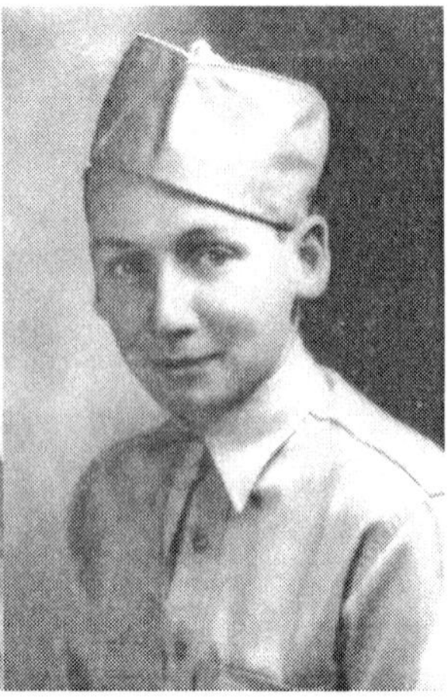

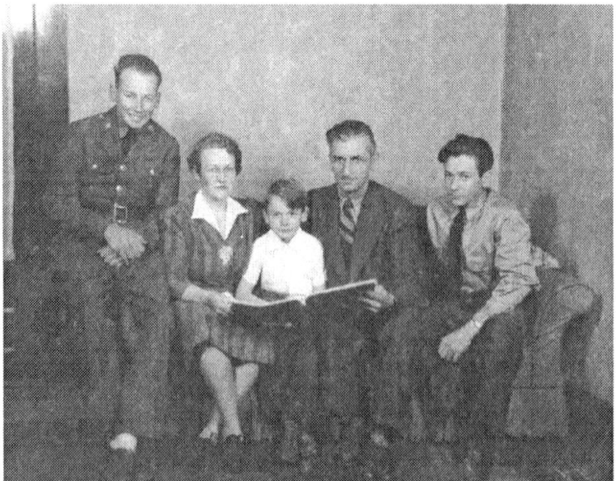

KETTER FAMILY

THE BLACK TRUNK

While doing research on Bronze Star recipient Maxwell Lee, I had an opportunity to obtain some rare one of a kind photographs of World War Two. While speaking, Max stated he wanted me to look at some newspaper articles he had compiled six years ago. Max had gone to the Republican newspaper and copied articles from 1944 and 1945. I agreed to look at them and went on my way amazed only by the photos Max was lending me. When I took the time that evening to look at the four inch stack of papers he had wanted me to see, it wasn't long before I realized that I had in front of me a window into the past.

The owner and editor of Danville, Indiana's Republican newspaper was Pug Weesner. Pug had a soft spot for our boys in uniform due to the fact he had fought in World War One. The pages were filled every week with updates on boys from Stilesville to North Salem and Plainfield to Brownsburg; it seems that if you were serving our country Pug kept tabs on you. From Pearl Harbor to V.J. Day the Republican was the county's message board. I was told that families would drop by with a recently received letter or told when a boy was home on leave. Promotions, draft notices, weddings and accounts of battle were posted every week in the pages of the local paper. I read that on Victory in Europe Day, the Danville Fire Department circled the courthouse ringing its bells and sounding its horn on a rainy Tuesday night. You could almost shut your eyes and see Norman Rockwell's America in the stories.

The pages of the Republican half a century ago were filled with triumph and tragedy. I read of Class Presidents, star athletes and former students of Central Normal College that were in combat in the Pacific and Europe. I read of how young Gene Oxley of the coast guard had been recognized for his actions at Omaha Beach. During the allied invasion Oxley's landing craft had become stuck on an obstacle one hundred yards off shore. The former Stilesville basketball star jumped overboard and swam through the most savage killing field of the war in an attempt to stretch a rescue line for the landing party trapped in his boat. Once on the beach and under incredible fire the small town boy from the heartland carried several wounded men off of beachhead to a rescue boat.

I was then brought to unimaginable sacrifice and sorrow while reading. Mr. and Mrs. Raymond Ketter of Danville had three sons Billy Ray 23, Jack Allen 20 and Harry 9. I read in the pages that tragically the youngest son 9-year-old Harry had drowned in a swimming hole north of Ellis Park in 1942. Raymond Ketter had served his country in World War I. Mrs. Beatrice Ketter was known about town because she headed up the local Red Cross Chapter during the war.

Pfc. Billy Ray Ketter enlisted in the army as his father did before him on his eighteenth birthday May 12th 1941. Billy Ray trained in the states until 1944 when he was assigned to the 51st Armored Infantry Division and was shipped to England. Billy Ray participated in the allied invasion of France in June 1944. Billy Ray was killed July 20th in the battle for St. Lo, France when his company spearheaded the allied breakout from the coastal region against the German Army.

The middle son Jack Allen Ketter who was a football and basketball player left Danville High School on his eighteenth birthday just as his father and big brother had done on October 20, 1943 to join the Marine Corps. While stationed in the south pacific Jack Allen participated in the invasion of Guam. In March 1945 Jack Allen was assigned to the third Marine Division during the invasion of Iwo Jima. The island was significant because the Americans could utilize the airfields to launch air strikes against main land Japan. On March 3rd Jack Allen was wounded after landing on the island but rejoined his company after being treated. During a short retreat Jack and four other Marines had dropped their weapons to go through enemy lines to rescue two wounded buddies. The four men had run through enemy fire to carry a Marine whom had been wounded the previous day. His eyes covered with bandages, the wounded Marine was seen wandering blindly in an attempt to make his way back to the American line. On March 7th Pfc. Jack Allen Ketter was killed on the deselect island which held such an enormous strategic position that the Japanese fought to the death to defend it. Six thousand Americans died during the battle for this tiny island only eight square miles in size. Of the young Marines fighting on Iwo Jima the Legendary Admiral Chester Nimetz stated "Uncommon valor was a common virtue".

Pvt. Dan O'Connell a fellow Marine and buddy had written a letter to Mr. & Mrs. Ketter that was received before the official notification was delivered. The letter told of Jacks death and expressed sorrow for the family's loss. The letter stated: "Although you have much sorrow you have much to be proud of. You had one of the finest sons, who gave his all without a whimper. He was not only a grand fellow he was also one of the finest soldiers." O'Connell closed by stating, "You may consider your life a failure but you are wrong. You and yours are the indispensable. You have made the greatest contribution to the cause of a free nation."

Three years after the war ended on May 1, 1948 the brothers who had died in opposite sides of the earth were brought home to Danville the place they had left on their 18th birthdays. Appropriately the brothers were laid to rest side by side with Brother Harry in the same soil they had given their lives to defend.

While researching this story I started by knowing only that a Hendricks County family named Ketter had lost two sons in the war but knew little more. When I attempted to locate pictures of these forgotten men I was unable to do so, other than faded copies from the Republican. One morning when I saw Max Gibbs I asked him if he had ever known of the Ketters.

With a surprised look in his eyes Max stated "Yes, I knew Jack". Max shared a story of how he and Jack would sneak into the apple orchard on Old North Salem Road and steal apples as youths. When I mentioned that people didn't remember the story of the Ketter family's sacrifice, referring to his generation Max snapped back "We remember".

Raymond Ketter passed away in 1975 and his wife followed in 1981, as far as I know thus ending the Ketter name in our county. The sacrifice made by this forgotten family was absolute and final. I have heard it said that the tragedy of war is that it robs us of what could have been. Perhaps Jack or Billy Ray would have become educators, businessman, civic leaders or simply your friend and neighbor.

Through word of mouth I was able to locate the home owned by the Ketters in the later part of their lives. The home that the boys grew up in still stands on Old North Salem Road. I met with the owner Jim Woodrum. Jim told me he had purchased the home in 1979. When he and his expecting wife Sharon moved in, a few of the Ketter family belongings remained. Unable to locate any family or friends, the Woodrums were forced to move the property out. Jim told me he found a black trunk containing hundreds of photographs and letters. The trunk was a porthole into the family's lives. Fortunately Jim Woodrum is a veteran himself and realized the importance of the contents and placed the trunk in his attack twenty years ago. Jim and his wife stated that they one day intend to donate the trunk to the County Museum. Jim and his son removed the trunk from the attack and invited me to come to their home and go through its contents.

Photographs of the Ketter sons and shots taken while Raymond Ketter served in World War 1 were inside. Letters and western union telegrams also remained. The rosary Beatrice Ketter carried with her to Mass at St. Mary's Church was found in a small box. It was obvious that in spite of the family's great sacrifice their faith never wavered.

I found a yellowed letter in a photo album. Billy wrote the letter to his mother June 28th just weeks after the invasion had began and while his unit was engaging the German Army in the Norman hedgerow country just inside the French coast. Billy had started his letter like all the others, "My Dearest Mother". Billy wrote of his plans for after the war. "I thought for a while I might try my luck at a little restaurant business." Billy than told of a letter he had received from Jack who was stationed on the other side of the earth and commented. "I guess I'm a lot like Jack, there are a lot of things I would like to see in this world. I have seen, and done a lot of things in this world. But the thing I most want to see now is my home and you and Dad and Jack." It was evident to me that the men who saved the world had the same dreams, fears and love for home that we have today. The letter was received in Danville on July 28th 1944 eight days after Billy's death in the battle for St. Lo, France.

On a warm September morning I took my three sons to the resting place of the Ketter family at the south cemetery. The marker on the grave of Billy had slid off its stand several inches, with that I realized they might not have been visited in some time. My sons and I placed flags on the brother's graves in a meager attempt to thank them for the freedom and liberty we now enjoy, but sometime take for granted. I looked on as my young sons watched the flags blow in the wind. I wandered if they would ever understand or appreciate that the young men who slept beneath these blades of grass, do so for their freedom.

Things haven't changed much in the half a century since Jack and Billy walked these same streets. Saint Mary's is still open for business. We still have the right to vote and speak freely. Those that survived the war feel the men that did not return are the only true heroes. I disagree; these men were all giants.

When learning the events surrounding this families sacrifice I was frustrated that I hadn't heard the story until I read it in a newspaper more than half a century old. We should never forget this family's sacrifice. Too much was given to us to ever forget them. After reading this, and learning of the events surrounding this proud and patriotic family you too can say, "We remember."

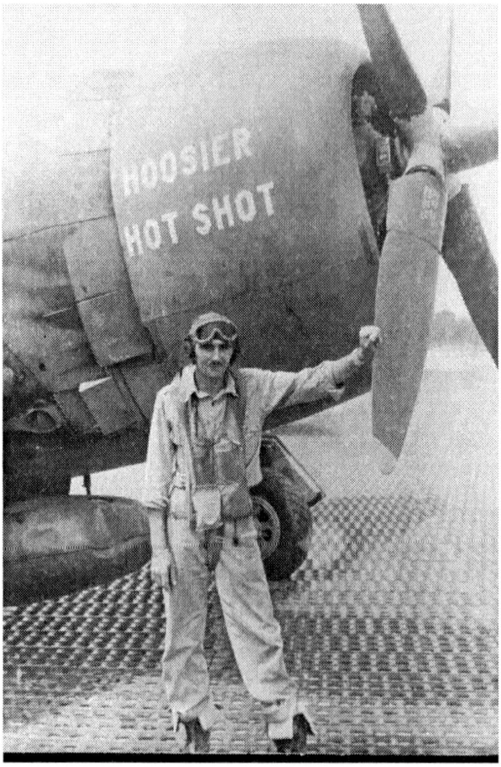
HOOSIER
HOT SHOT

LYNN PARSONS

HOOSIER HOT SHOT

The Parsons are similar to many families in the Midwest. They keep in touch by phone and meet every year or so for a reunion. The ringleader of the family reunion is Charles Parsons of Florida. He plans some of the events and finds out who is coming and who is not. He also acts as the family historian. In 1995 Charles came up with an idea to preserve one of the Parson family's proudest times ... the time when Uncle Lynn Parsons served in the Army Air Corps. He suggested using a video recorder to interview Uncle Lynn about his World War II service and Uncle Lynn agreed.

Lynn, 77 at the time, was videoed in his home in Brownsburg, Indiana. He sat in his favorite brown recliner while Charles asked the questions. Even though Lynn's eyesight was failing, his mind was as sharp as the days he had served his country. With a few sheets of paper in one hand and a magnifying glass in the other to read the notes he had prepared for the interview, Lynn told his nephew the story of his youth ... a story filled with daring, humor and personal events that helped change the world.

Lynn graduated from high school in 1937 and took a job at a local filling station and another at the Lizton Lumber Yard. In December 1940 he was drafted into the United States Army. America was at peace. "I was going to serve a year with an artillery unit." A year later when his service obligation was nearly up, his plans were changed along with millions like him. On December 7, 1941, Lynn's one-year obligation was extended indefinitely.

While stationed in Michigan, Lynn and 20 others from his unit were sent to Detroit to pick up a shipment of new jeeps.

Daniel Webster, a friend who had just joined the Army Air Forces, greeted Lynn there. "At the time, you needed to have two years of college or pass an exam to get assigned as a pilot," Lynn told his nephew during the interview. "Webster said he had studied for the test and that I could come to his house and he would help me." Lynn did just that and only days later passed the exam, was given a physical the same day, and that evening was sworn in to the United States Army Air Forces. "It all just gelled at once," Lynn stated. He returned to his artillery unit the following Monday, and his new orders arrived on Wednesday. "My First Sergeant was awful mad when he saw those orders, but there was nothing he could do about it. They needed pilots bad."

He moved to Oklahoma City for his primary training then on to Enid, Oklahoma, for basic training and took his advanced training in Lake Charles, Louisiana. Lynn's flight training was at still-under-construction Kelly Field in San Antonio, Texas. He was assigned to the 348th Fighter Group at Bradley Field, Connecticut, when his training was completed. "We didn't know what we were getting into when they sent us there." Lynn's fighter group would be piloting a new aircraft known as the Republic P-47 Thunderbolt.

Just 30 days before the 348th was to be shipped to Europe, the Pacific commanders made a plea to President Roosevelt. "They told him if they didn't have more pilots in the Pacific, the Japanese would invade Australia." Instead of Europe, the 348th was dispatched to the Pacific. On June 14, 1943, Lynn arrived in Brisbane, Australia. "On July 24 we arrived at Port Moresby. It was quite interesting. The natives had all of their buildings up on stilts about 12 or 15 feet high. I had never seen anything like that before," Lynn told his nephew. When the P-47 arrived that would be assigned to Lynn, he decided to give it a name. "Hoosier Hot Shot" was boldly painted on the nose of the aircraft.

Lynn flew his first combat mission on July 29 1943. "In those early days, we mostly flew ground support, strafing and dive bombing. Once in a while we flew bomber support, but our range was limited," Lynn stated. He told his nephew that he had flown for a long time before he saw his first enemy aircraft and this frustrated him. "You know when you take a fighter outfit, they're pretty high strung. You actually want to get in a fight. It's a pretty big thrill. I never realized that fighter pilots were that way until we had a mission briefing with our bomber pilots. Those guys were just the opposite; they were scared. It's probably because they were sitting ducks." Lynn flew his first big mission on September 5. His squadron escorted eight troop transports carrying paratroopers. They landed in Martin Valley on New Guinea. "The mission was real successful. We didn't lose any planes that day."

"On Tuesday, September the 21st, the Japs bombed Port Moresby. It was the first time we had been bombed since we arrived." In October Lynn was moved to the 460th Fighter Squadron based out of Tacloban in the Philippines. While recalling his experiences in the Philippines, Lynn told his nephew a humorous story. "It was the rainy season; everything was soaking wet. We were sitting around in our tent one day and water was running through the floor. I looked down and saw a half-full bottle of whisky floating through the tent. I grabbed it, pulled open the top and we chugged it."

Even though Lynn had seen only action from bombing and strafing, he still had his share of close calls. While on patrol over Leyte on December 2, 1944, his aircraft experienced engine failure. "My first impulse was to bail out. I decided to stay with it. I saw an inlet between the mountains. I circled around and landed on an airstrip." Just eight days later, Lynn was able to find the fight he was itching for. While leading a patrol of four P-47s over Ormoc Bay at Leyte, Lynn sighted a lone Japanese bomber. He pursued it and fired a long burst from his guns. The enemy aircraft was struck and crashed into the Philippine Sea.

On December 12 Lynn was again leading his squadron near Leyte when they were sent to intercept a Japanese shipping convoy approaching the island. Lynn gave the order for six of the aircraft to attack the ships. He, along with another fighter, attacked a destroyer. "I dropped both my bombs but they missed. We then circled around and opened fire on the destroyer with our eight 50-caliber machine guns. When we passed over, we could see the deck disintegrating." The destroyer returned fire and hit Lynn's wingman. Lynn made several runs at the ship with his guns blazing. The encounter was ferocious; guns from the Japanese destroyer were firing point blank at Lynn's aircraft as he dove at the enemy. When he pulled away, the ship was adrift and on fire. Lynn's wingman was forced to crash into the sea. "He was picked up by a PBY and made it back to base before I did," Lynn stated with a laugh.

Lynn engaged two Japanese aircraft on another occasion, repeatedly striking one. The wounded plane ducked under a nearby cloudbank with Lynn in hot pursuit. When Lynn emerged from the clouds, he saw the enemy aircraft with another P-47 on its tail. The enemy plane was then shot down. Lynn shrugged his shoulders and stated, "I didn't get credit for that one."

While serving in the campaign, Lynn's heroics had been noticed by his commanders. He was promoted to the rank of Captain. He was the recipient of five air medals and also one of our nation's top military decorations, the Distinguished Flying Cross with Oak Leaf Cluster. He flew a total of 230 missions.

Lynn experienced his last close call of the war in the winter of 1944. Due to a faulty gauge, his aircraft ran out of fuel. Despite this he was able to make an emergency landing. His commander told him his luck had run out and he was grounded. He declined another promotion and was sent back to the States.

In the summer of 1945, Lynn volunteered as a test pilot at Wright Patterson Air Base, Dayton, Ohio. He and a fellow pilot tested the first automatic pilot system for fighters. "They wanted us to put 100 hours on the system." During some test flights, Lynn flew over his hometown. "I would buzz Brownsburg and the lumber company in Lizton." Lynn would go into a dive at 500 miles an hour before passing over the towns. There was little chance he would be reprimanded for this. After all, no one would know who was terrifying these small towns. "I had the number 48 painted on the nose of the plane. It was kind of small and I didn't think anyone could see it. While on leave one weekend, I hitched a ride to Brownsburg. I started to walk into a café one day when a young boy stopped me at the door. He asked, 'How's 48 running today?'"

Lynn left the military after the war ended and the "Hoosier Hot Shot" returned to his job at the Lizton Lumber Yard. I find it fascinating that the men who fought in World War II could put their war experiences behind them. They had spent a great deal of their young lives on the ragged edge. Adrenaline and emotions had fueled them. Regardless, most were able to take off their uniforms, hang them in their closets and never look back. They returned to civilian jobs chocked full of routine and hard work. Even though they were young, they had accomplished a great deal. During his duties in the Pacific, Lynn Parsons had experienced enough high drama to last him his lifetime. Lynn continued to work at the same lumber company. He liked his work so much, he eventually purchased the Lizton Lumber Yard.

The video Charles Parsons taped of his uncle's experiences lasts about an hour. "I made it because it is an important part of my family's history. I didn't want it to be lost," Charles told me. Copies of the video have been distributed to family members. Charles was correct: by taking a few hours of his time to videotape his uncle, the World War II experiences of the "Hoosier Hot Shot" have been captured and preserved in Lynn Parson's own words.

"He was always a hero to my brother and me. During the war, I was eight years old. There was a certain prestige that came with having an uncle that was a fighter pilot. He was one of the elite," Charles recalls. "He has a high standing in our family of over 100 scattered throughout the country."

Watching the video in the Brownsburg home of Lynn Parsons was a treat for me. The tape is simply an older man sitting in his favorite recliner telling stories to his nephew. While the tape played, I caught a glimpse of Charles still riveted to his uncle's every word. Then it occurred to me the true reason the recording came about ... it is apparent that the "Hoosier Hot Shot" once was and always will be his hero.

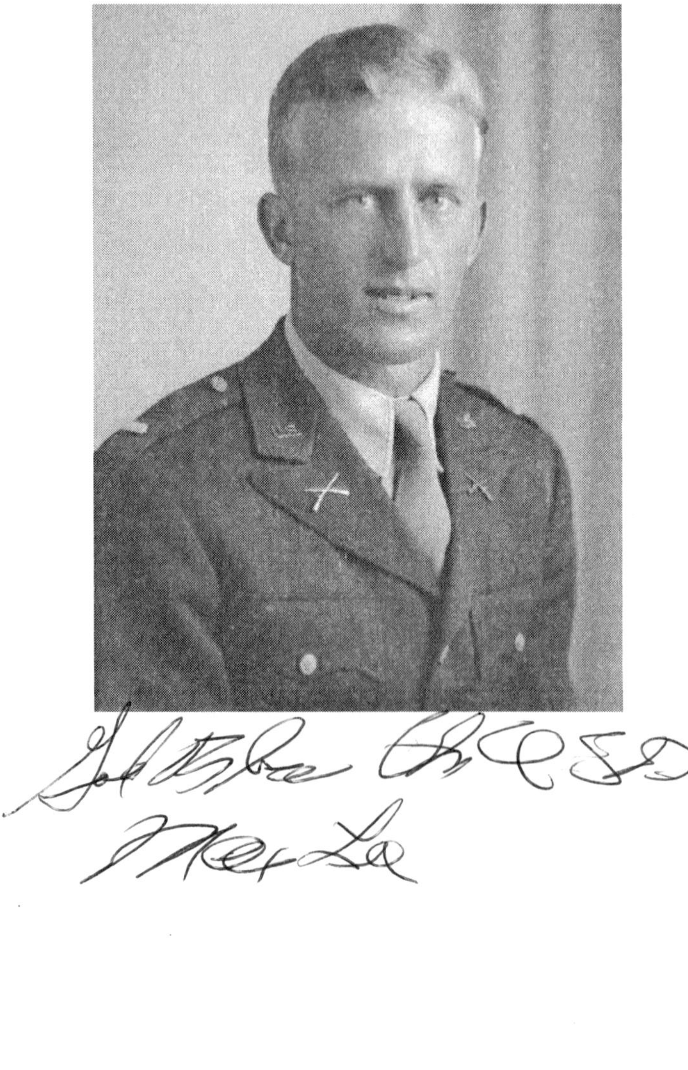

MAX LEE

THE WAR YEARS

Max Lee is an eighty-one year old gentleman whom you'll find most mornings at the Danville Hardee's. After spending thirty years working as the postmaster of our local post office. Max now spends most of his time running errands for his wife. Max lives the typical life for a retired man his age with one exception—he's still a First Lieutenant in the United States Army. For some reason, he's never been discharged. The following is a story of a great warrior, a grateful American, and the men he once trusted with his life.

About a year ago my good friend, Lyle Springer, introduced me to Max Lee. You see Lyle is our local barber. He knows just about every one and everyone's story. I guess being a barber in a small town like Danville gives you time to explore your clients' lives and histories. Sitting around the barbershop is still something that's done in the heartland. I have even found myself stopping by to sit and chat on occasion without stepping a foot near Lyle's tattered chair. Lyle told me that Max Lee was wounded in World War II and that he would be a great person to talk with. Lyle didn't know a great deal more than he was a tank commander and that he had a Purple Heart plate on his Oldsmobile van.

In August I encountered Max Lee while he was sitting on a bench at the Danville Kroger's. I told him I had started a new hobby and asked if we could talk some time. Max agreed and with his gruff voice, he announced that he had once written his memoirs and that I could take a look at his last remaining copy. I have found it rare that veterans have taken the time to write their memoirs. Who knows the reasons? Maybe memories have faded, things that happened nearly sixty years ago remain still too painful to speak of, or they don't believe that their link to one of histories most pivotal times is important to anyone now.

Max's memoirs are 13 typed pages of heroism, togetherness, and sacrifice titled THE WAR YEARS by Max Lee. I read about how the twenty-one year old worked his way back from California to Danville in 1940 to be drafted in his home state.

He wrote of his training in the States and how they received the word that the U.S. was at war. Max related that he had enlisted as a private but was a first lieutenant by the time he was stationed in Europe. He talks about the boat ride across the Atlantic. Almost every veteran first talks about the ride over-- one can only imagine what a five or six-day trip on a crowded troop ship would be like. Max stated he ate a lot of fish, even at breakfast.

Not long after being in Europe, Lt. Lee was assigned to the 84th Infantry Division. On December 16, 1944, the Germans made their last great offensive drive against the Allies in the Ardennes Forest. The battle would be known as "the Battle of the Bulge." Historians would write that the American forces were outnumbered eight to one when the Germans attacked. Max wrote in his memoirs that he thought to himself, *now is the time to be a soldier.* The enemy was coming at us, direction unknown. Then Max made a statement that would be the overlying theme of his memoirs and oral history. "I would join the men who I would trust with my life, and they with mine," he wrote. Few of us will ever know or understand the total bond and trust that formed between these soldiers as they tried to conquer evil on a land far from home.

Assigned to the 334th Regiment of the 84th Division during the battle, he would be in command of four tanks, two scout cars and a jeep known as the flying cloud. Lt. Lee also had two P-51 aircraft with artillery support if called for. During the battle, his group lost two tanks and several men were wounded. Max wrote that orders were carried out quickly and accurately carried out. Not only did he and his men endure the

German attacks, but they also had to survive the extreme cold. While trying to survive the battle, he learned to quickly trust each of his men. Two men, Sgt. Kash and Sgt. Westfal, became close to him. This bond would last throughout the campaign. When riding in a jeep, Lee states, that 6'9" tall Staff Sgt. Kash looked like he was standing up. Sgt. Kash was from Dayton, Ohio, and was married with a child.

The 84ths orders were to beat the advancing German army to the town of Marche, Belgium. The small town had to be captured and defended at all costs. Marche had inside its limits a crucial crossroad, if the Germans had captured the small town first, they would have access to allied fuel supplies. The fuel would have allowed their powerful panzer and tiger tank divisions to advance the offensive north separating the British and American armies during the surprise attack. After taking Marche the 84th was surrounded. Max wrote that his unit would fire a few shots at the Germans, score a hit or two and than hide. The lifeless bodies of both American and German soldiers lied all along the frozen streets. Marche was held and the spearhead of the Nazi army was stopped and unable to re-supply.

During the fighting Lt. Lee's company moved into a burning town overlooking a stream. Lee said that several German vehicles started moving toward his position from a wooded area. Lee's unit started firing, setting one of the enemy vehicles on fire, and causing the others to turn away. One German tank continued straight on. The tank suddenly became stuck in the creek spinning its track. Lt. Lee said a fellow lieutenant who had been a New York City policeman suggested they attempt to knock the tank out with a bazooka. Lt. Lee, along with his fellow lieutenant, moved up on the tank. Two shots at the tracks had failed to damage the tank. It was then that the lieutenant yelled at Lee, "Get up there," and boosted him onto the back of the tank. Lee fired one shot into the ventilator causing the engine to stop. It was then that he noticed the hatch opening. "I threw a grenade in the opening and jumped on the hatch," Lee said. The SS Tiger tank was still there the next morning.

When speaking of the fellow lieutenant, whose name he can't remember, a grin comes to his face. "Man that guy wasn't scared of nothing. While out on patrol one night, he and I ate at a German chow line. The Germans didn't want to cause any disturbances so they let us go. You should have seen the looks on their faces. We ate something like biscuits and gravy. It wasn't very good but it was hot," Lee said with a smile. When they got back to the unit and told the others what they had done, they were met with disbelief. "Well, we're not hungry are we?" was the only evidence they had. Lee did tell his fellow lieutenant that would be the last time he went anywhere with him. Lee shakes his head and says he was as cool as a cucumber. "I learned that he was later killed in action."

Shortly after Christmas, 1944, the tide had turned in the Battle of the Bulge. The German army's last great offensive had failed due to men like Lt. Lee, Sgt. Kash, Sgt. Westfall, a fearless New York City policeman, along with countless other GIs who stood their ground when the battle to liberate Europe hung in the balance. Lee's unit paid a heavy price during the surprise Nazi attack. Lee had shown me a unit photograph with dozens of Xs next to those killed. Lee would write, "While enduring the cold, lack of food and sleep the enemy popping up everywhere an unsaid unity in spirit was formed between us that would last for years, it was stronger than brotherhood. The bond would see us through no matter what we faced."

After the battle, the 84th was given its orders to move toward Berlin, the German capital. While moving across a stream, Lt. Lee saw a German 88, which is an artillery gun. Lee, on foot alongside a tank, noticed a squad of German soldiers about to man the gun. He stated that a separate gun started firing at him from a house. Lt. Lee threw a grenade at the 88, knocking it out of action. When Lee returned, he found that he had been wounded. As Lee laughs about it, he says, "A colonel had been watching us." Lt. Lee was awarded the

Bronze Star "for heroism in ground combat" and the Purple Heart.

One early morning at Hardee's, Max Lee told me that the Bronze Star was nothing. "The most important thing we did was when Sgt. Kash, Cpl. Stratton, and I were out alone and found two German soldiers near a railroad track. They surrendered to us with white flags. Cpl. Stratton, who was an interpreter, questioned them and found that the woods ahead of us were full of German troops." With Lt. Lee on the right side of the road and Sgt. Kash on the left, the trio led the two captured Nazis down the middle of the road. The Germans were told to start yelling at their comrades to surrender. "When we crested the hill, we encountered a large column of Germans coming toward us in combat formation. The captured Germans kept yelling surrender. The men in the column put their guns down and raised their hands. Sgt. Kash turned the mounted machine gun on the men, and the three of us led the large column of captured men back to town behind our jeep. Instead of getting a medal when I got back, I was reprimanded for giving a German officer a cigarette," Lee said with a laugh.

Max Lee speaks and writes of his final moments in combat. In his memoirs, this chapter is simply titled: *A life saved, A life lost.* On April 7, 1945, Lt. Lee was to lead two tanks across an open field to penetrate a dug-in enemy position. Infantry would follow his tanks on foot. While moving across the field, Lee noticed that the infantry was no longer with him. It was then he noticed a German artillery gun swinging around to take aim at his tank. Lee said, "I told the sergeant with me we had to fire at the gun. That was the last thing I remember," said Lee. "We were hit with a shell, and all four men in the tank were killed." Because he was up top of the open tank, he was thrown clear of the burning wreckage. "I came to lying on my back when I suddenly felt someone pulling at my legs. I made an attempt to pull my .45 when I realized it was Sgt Kash." Sgt. Kash had run from cover into the open area to pull his lieutenant to safety. Kash yelled to Lee that he was taking him back. Just than Kash was shot to death. Lee stated he then passed out and awoke in a field hospital. Lee was seriously injured and would require several surgeries and rehabilitation to recover.

While speaking of this selfless act of heroism nearly sixty years later, Max Lee had a distant expression in his eyes. These men, some of them fresh out of high school, had created a bond so intense that risking or laying down your own life for a buddy was something done without hesitation. In my readings, I have heard it told that most veterans fought, bled and died not for flag or country but for their buddies and the men they were serving with. Sgt. Kash, the tall soldier from Ohio who had died trying to rescue his lieutenant, was awarded the Silver Star posthumously. Lt. Lee said he corresponded with Kash's family when he returned home to the States.

I met Max Lee for breakfast recently. While talking Max said theirs one thing I left out in my story. "We were going in to a town during the battle, the rain was falling lightly as we entered. The Germans were shelling us very heavy and I was scared. I jumped in a ditch and rolled over on my back. I remember looking up at the gray sky above me. It was then that I saw a large white cross next to me. Suddenly a calm came over me; I got out of the ditch gathered my men and we continued the battle. I told Sgt. Kash about the cross, after the fighting was over I returned to show it to him and it was gone." Who knows what Max saws in this moment of need maybe it was a figment of his imagination, or was it something else? You the reader can be the judge.

If you are a veteran of any campaign, take the time to record your memories so that your feats--no matter how trivial or spectacular--won't be lost. The value of Max Lee's memoirs and his oral history goes beyond telling future generations about dates and places. It tells us that at one time, men bonded and sacrificed. We owe them all a profound debt of gratitude. Some of these heroes still walk among us. I should know, I saw one at breakfast.

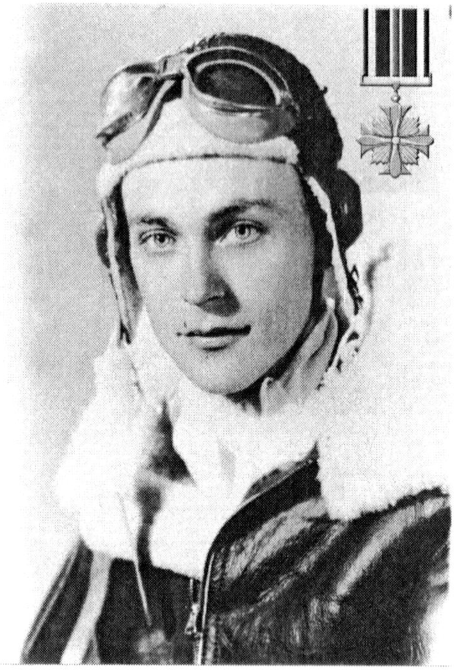

CHARLIE PERRY

TRUE SURVIVOR

Survivor is a designation made popular by a recent television show. People volunteer to be placed on a desert island in hopes of being rewarded a million dollars. Difficult, yes, but a true test of survival? I don't think so. The following is a definition of this word's true meaning.

While having a talk with Dr. William Strother, pastor of the Northview Christian Church, I was told of Charlie Perry. Dr. Strother told me of Perry's amazing story during World War II. Charlie's phone number was provided straight out of the church directory and I quickly made arrangements to meet with Charlie at his home near CR 200 North. I found Charlie Perry to be a humble man with a quick wit and an engaging since of humor. Charlie retired from farming and at one time owned his own kitchen counter company. Charlie and his wife Zella retired two years ago as tax specialist. Charlie found success in the business world and was spending time volunteering for his Church. The Perrys have called Hendricks County home for twenty years. While in the Perry home, I was introduced to his entire family via photographs on the mantle. Charlie beamed with pride when he spoke of his daughter, Donna. "It was always our dream for Donna to attend Purdue University." Donna graduated with a degree, and now Charlie's grandson is a Boilermaker.

Charlie Perry grew up on the eastside of Indianapolis during the Great Depression. Perry told me of how his mother had passed away when he was a small child. One of Charlie's sisters died not long after. His father tried to hold the family of three girls and one boy together but contracted tuberculosis when Charlie was nine. While his father battled the disease, young Charlie and his sisters were placed in a foster home. Charlie speaks fondly of the family that practically raised him and his sisters. "The Cottons were 65 years old when they took us in. Can you imagine being that old and volunteering to raise four kids?" I commented to Charlie that his life sounded rough. Charlie shook his head and said, "No, it was my dad who had it rough."

Charlie Perry, drafted in 1942 and given a draft-board physical, told the doctors about his mother's death and his father's condition. Charlie stated, "They stamped me 4-F," (which means medically unfit) "and let me leave." Like millions of others who couldn't fight for medical reasons, Charlie was disappointed and restless. The sense of duty and wanting to do your part was astounding during that era. He went back to the local induction office and tried to volunteer. "This time I didn't answer all those questions quite as honestly, and I was accepted," Charlie told me with a grin.

Charlie Perry completed basic training, went to Salt Lake City where he was assigned to the 706th Squadron of the 446th Bomber Group, and was assigned to a ten-man, B-24 bomber crew. The B-24 was an aircraft with four engines. Maximum range was 2100 miles with speed of 300 mph. "Our Officers were good guys; they didn't try to pull rank on you like other officers did," Charlie commented. The ten men became a team as close as any family.

Charlie's crew was sent to Florida in August of 1943, waiting orders to join the fighting. Charlie was unsure if they would be sent to the Pacific Theater or Europe. An hour into the air, Captain Charles Mckeny opened a sealed envelope to find that they were to fly to England.

The 446th was assigned to the legendary Eighth Air Force, responsible for a majority of the bombing raids over Nazi-held Europe. The Eighth experienced an extremely high casualty rate. The bombing missions in 1943-44 were designed to interrupt the German war machine's ability to produce aircraft, fuel and transportation systems. The Allies knew that they must weaken the German's capabilities before an invasion of France would be possible. Hitler's stranglehold over the continent was absolute.

Charlie was a ball-turret gunner. The ball turret was a small capsule located on the belly of the aircraft. As the belly gunner, it was Charlie's job to fend off enemy aircraft. Charlie kept records of each of his 29 missions, which he allowed me to read. Each mission was filled with heroism and adventure. Charlie flew his first bombing mission on Christmas Eve, 1943. After a sleepless night, Charlie Perry and his crew boarded a B-24 bomber named "Shiflus Skunk." The mission was to bomb a rocket installation at Eclimax, France. The mission was uneventful; the "Shiflus Skunk" along with other bombers of the 446th hit their target and returned safely to base.

Six days later the crew flew its second mission. This mission would be more indicative of the challenge that lay ahead. The target was a chemical factory at Ludswighaven, Germany. Near the target, the 446th met anti-aircraft fire and 15 German fighters. Charlie's crew witnessed an American aircraft shot down with only two of ten parachutes seen. Charlie's crew continued on its mission and safely returned to base. Not only were the bomber crews facing anti-aircraft guns, enemy aircraft, and engine failure, they were also forced to survive the elements. Flying at 25,000 feet in an unpressurized aircraft is a dangerous task. The temperatures dropped 30-40 degrees below zero and oxygen was scarce. Charlie said that, while under fire from anti-aircraft guns and attack by the Luftwaffe, on more than one occasion he saw a member of the crew frozen at his guns. Charlie said that under the stress of combat, men would create a seal on their oxygen masks causing the moisture around their mouths to freeze. Ice would form and men would lose consciousness. Charlie said a fellow crewmember had this happen twice. Charlie left his guns to break the mask free. Charlie would place his oxygen supply on the man's face until he would come around.

The crew flew many more missions into heavily defended German territory. On January 24, a mission was flown to bomb the Nazi rail yards at Frankfurt, Germany. En route to the target, the 446th encountered heavy flack. The black bursts of exploding German shells reached up into the sky 20,000 feet randomly picking off Allied planes flying in defensive formation. During the missions, it was a matter of life or death to remain in your formation. While flying in formation, the aircraft were better able to defend themselves against enemy fighters. If an aircraft was damaged or experienced engine trouble, it was forced to slow and drop from the formation. Much like lions on the African plains, the Germans would feast on the weak and defenseless stragglers when they left the safety of the herd. On this mission, Charlie's aircraft experienced power loss in all four engines. Captain Mckeny was able to keep in formation as the group dropped its payload on the railway. After the bombs were dropped on the target, a dash was made for the English Channel. Charlie's crew looked on helplessly as four Allied aircraft were shot down. While being pursued west, the crew could see black smoke spiraling over the horizon behind them. Captain Mckeny safely guided "Shiflus Skunk" back to base. While talking with Charlie, the admiration and affection he felt for his 24-year old captain is obvious. "Our entire crew was as close as any family. For nine months we ate, slept head-to-head, and went through battle together."

On January 4, another mission to Frankfurt was flown. As before, American aircraft were lost and Charlie's aircraft was repeatedly hit. Luck and skill brought the "Shiflus Skunk" home each time. This was Sgt. Charlie Perry's sixth mission. He would be required to fly 23 more. The three months it would take to complete the tour must have seemed like an eternity.

Anxieties were high among these young men. On March 3, 1944, the 446th gathered for the usual mission brief when a map of the German capital, Berlin, was uncovered. Charlie stated that moans came from the crews and a few men became ill. Berlin was heavily defended by a system of anti-aircraft guns and fighter squadrons. One can only imagine what crossed the minds of those men sitting in the room that day nearly 60 years ago. Casualties were sure to be high. Would it be a buddy from another crew? Or would it be you that didn't come back for the nightly poker game in the barracks? Fate smiled on Charlie Perry that day; the mission was recalled over Holland due to bad weather.

Charlie's crew flew many more missions until April, 1944. Each bombing raid was necessary to the war effort, but countless aircraft were lost in these months. Near the end of April, Sgt. Charlie Perry was to finish his tour and be reassigned as an instructor either in England or the States. Charlie told me that he had even requested and been fitted with a new pair of GI shoes to wear when he went on leave.

On April 29, 1944, Charlie volunteered to be a replacement gunner for another bombing crew. The B-24 was named "Luck and Stuff." This would be his 29th and final bombing mission. The target would be Berlin. Charlie asked the tail gunner, Jimmy Calhoun, to switch places with him. Calhoun denied Charlie's request. Charlie recalled the sky was beautiful that day. After the bombs were dropped, flack hit "Luck and Stuff." Two of the engines were damaged on the B-24, and the ten-man crew was forced to drop from the protection of the formation. The squadron left "Luck and Stuff" behind as she was losing altitude and speed. Forty-five minutes west of Berlin, fighter escorts were radioed to cover the wounded craft. Minutes later several German fighters (FW 190's), intercepting the call for help, appeared. The enemy quickly attacked the defenseless aircraft. In the first pass, Jimmy Calhoun was killed. Another member of the crew was struck in the leg. Fuel tanks ignited and fire raged inside the aircraft killing the flight engineer. The order was made to abandon the plane. The eight remaining crewmembers parachuted from the aircraft as it was under attack. Charlie jumped through a hatch at the nose of the aircraft as it started to nose-dive. One of the wounded aviators did not survive the jump. Charlie commented that after free falling, he opened his chute only to find that he was being circled by one of the enemy planes. Charlie played dead hoping the enemy wouldn't shoot him as he floated to earth. "Luck & Stuff" exploded before it hit the ground.

The Indiana boy, on his last mission and only hours from getting his ticket home, found himself on the ground hundreds of miles behind enemy lines. As he was trained, Charlie removed his chute and hid it under some brush. When he turned to run, much to his dismay he saw 100 angry German civilians surrounding him with clubs and pitchforks. In the crowd were two German soldiers. The mob would surely kill the Americans; the only chance was to run to the soldiers. Charlie, unarmed and dazed, surrendered to the pair and was led away. Just hours away from wearing his new shoes home, Charlie Perry found himself on enemy soil, a thousand miles from England and a world away from Indiana. Charlie Perry would now face a second fight for survival, as he was lead away to a Prisoner of War camp.

After being interrogated Charlie was loaded onto a freight car with other Allied prisoners. Charlie stated, "I could see through a crack in the boxcar. I could see the destruction we had caused during our bombing missions." Charlie could see a single church steeple, which remained undamaged. The crowded train took the Allied prisoners on a four-day trip to Heydekrug, East Prussia. During the train ride, Charlie met another Allied airman named Snuffy Stewart. The men became close friends and have kept in touch over the past 56 years. It's amazing how these men, who spent a relatively short period of their lives together, created such a strong bond that they became life-long friends.

Once at the German prison camp, Charlie was assigned a number: 3714. After a few days at the camp and after convincing the other prisoners that he wasn't a spy, the camp escape committee approached Charlie. He was told that the committee must approve any escape attempt.

Back in the States, Charlie's family had been notified by the War Department that Charlie's aircraft had been shot down and that Charlie and his crew were officially "missing in action." It wasn't until a group of ham radio operators overheard German propaganda broadcasts that information about his fate was known. Charlie Perry's name was given during a nightly Axes Sally show. The ham radio operator mailed a postcard to Charlie's father to tell of what he had heard.

Around July 4, 1944, Charlie stated they could hear the artillery from the advancing Russian army. Hitler's once invincible war machine was gradually losing ground.

In early July, the POWs were ordered out of their barracks and led away to the seaport at Memel. The men were loaded onto a coal freighter named the Mauserin. The ship had a capacity of 500 men but over 2,000 were forced aboard.

Conditions were unbearable during the 36-hour journey. One POW jumped overboard in an attempt to escape, but German guards opened fire on him. Charlie never learned the man's fate. When the ship docked, the tired men were once again loaded onto freight cars and transported near the town of Stargaard. The men were ordered to line up along a roadway. It was then that Charlie's morale hit rock bottom. The men were ordered to run five miles through the woods to the camp. Charlie states that dogs and guards with bayonets chased them. One of the men who fell behind was bayoneted by the guards and bitten by the dogs. His buddies carried him the remainder of the way. He had been stabbed 60 times but survived. At the new camp, prisoners were given only a small amount of bread, coffee and grass soup for lunch. Dinner consisted of a single baked potato.

After a few short months at the camp, the roar of the approaching Russian army could be heard in the distance. Once again orders were given to evacuate the men. This time trains and ships would not be provided. Eleven thousand men were sent on a desperate march in the dead of winter. Food was scarce during the march. One would think that all hope must have been lost. Charlie Perry told me that, in spite of the dangers he had faced in the air and as a Prisoner of War, he always knew he would live. "I always knew I would make it home somehow." If placed in Charlie's situation, what would we do? The easiest thing to do would be to give up hope. The choice to remain strong and push forward would be more difficult than lying down on the frozen ground to perish or force the guards to open fire during a futile escape attempt.

It was now March 1945. The Allied armies and the Russians were closing in on the German fatherland. The POWs would encounter German civilians on their forced journey. The roads were packed with civilians trying to escape the Russians. The POWs received a morale boost when they were told to lie in ditches next to the roadway as a column of retreating German tanks roared passed. Charlie stated a few of the Scottish soldiers taunted the Germans by defiantly playing their bagpipes.

On April 27, 1945, the men were led to an abandoned ceramics factory near the Elbe River. The POWs were held in the dark factory overnight. In the middle of the night, two American soldiers dressed in civilian clothing slipped past the guards and entered the factory through a window. Here were the rescuers that the beleaguered men had prayed for appearing like thieves in the night. The pair told them that their unit was poised on the other side of the Elbe River and that, if the Germans had not surrendered the POWs in the morning, they intended to assault the building and bring them back. How would this journey into hell end for the tired, defenseless men? Would they be handed over peacefully, or would they be unarmed bystanders in a bloody rescue attempt? The hours before dawn must have seemed like an eternity. Early the next morning, the POWs were marched to a bombed-out bridge over the Elbe River. They were then told to march across. Charlie vividly recalls his last few steps of captivity. "As I was walking across the bridge, I could see an American soldier standing there. I couldn't tell you what he looked like. All I could see were his gold second lieutenant bars. I wept as I walked past the lieutenant. I was given a Bible that I still have." The awaiting Americans met Charlie and the others on the other side of the bridge.

I was invited into Charlie's home to talk about his experience. I have spoken with several World War II veterans and have had the privilege to be invited into their homes. One thing I have found that most of these men have in common is a small room tucked away from the rest of the house. While in Charlie Perry's study, I saw a picture frame unassumingly placed in a corner near the bookshelf. Upon closer examination, I saw that the frame contained the Distinguished Flying Cross, one of our nation's highest decorations for valor and conduct in combat. Charlie hadn't acknowledged the medal until I saw it. It was awarded to Charlie Perry Stout Field while he was still a Prisoner of War.

Charlie was known for his humor. In December of 2000 I gathered some of the men in this book for breakfast. Many of them had never met. I didn't know what to expect once they were gathered. I broke the ice by having the men introduce their self. Once the introductions were complete, the stories started to fly. I was riveted to every word. When I stopped to look around the restaurants I found I wasn't alone several other patrons had stopped eating and were listening in. The stories flew from one veteran to the next. Finally Harry Northern stated, "Are we going to order breakfast?" Without missing a beat Charlie nudged Harry in the side and said, "We haven't won the war yet."

On March 12 2001 I received a call from Zella, Charlie had passed away unexpectedly. At his crowded funeral service Dr. Billy Strother stated "Charlie Perry loved his Country, his Family and his Lord." Dr. Strother then compared Charlie's passing to the incident fifty-six years ago when he crossed a bridge over the Elbe River to return home. During the service Dr. Strother stated "Did you know Charlie was a veteran?" The question was met with a roar of laughter. Charlie was proud of his accomplishments and we were all proud of him. Charlie had lived a remarkable life. Few have ever squeezed as much tragedy and triumph into a lifetime. When Zella called to tell me of Charlie's passing I was quite saddened. My wife comforted me when she said, "Your life is better because you knew him." She was right, I know all of our lives are better because of the cabinetmaker, farmer, tax specialist, and hero who sacrificed to make our land free.

RALPH W COOPER

RALPH COOPER

MARATHON

Ralph Cooper hails from Dugger, a tiny town in southern Indiana, and is one of four kids. He graduated from high school in Terra Haute and then went on to work in a cigar store and a paint company. At age 22, he walked into a recruiter's office to volunteer and began his military service on February 10, 1941, ten months before Pearl Harbor.

Ralph was stationed at Fort Benning, Georgia. It was near the end of his first year of service that he heeded the advice of a fellow soldier who thought he should train as a medic. Medical training was conducted near Fort Benning at a site known as the "Harmony Church Area." Ralph isn't sure why he decided to transfer to the medical unit. He most likely just wanted to take on a new challenge and learn a new skill.

Ralph was assigned to the 2nd Armored Division. The 2nd Armored Division had a nickname they were quite proud of: "Hell on Wheels." In 1942 Ralph was teamed with the 17th Engineers Regiment of the 2nd Armored Division. They were destined to be among the first to engage the Germans in battle in the deserts of North Africa. Within days of landing in Casablanca, the regiment came under German rocket attack.

As Ralph talked about those days in North Africa, he showed me a stack of small black and white photographs. Ralph's good friend, Sgt. Fink, took most of the photos. Fink was from Chicago. "He was a great guy," Ralph said about Fink. The photos Fink had taken long ago captured images of African children as well as members of the 2nd Armored Division.

American and British forces faced the German army at one of its strongest times. At Kasserine Pass, Field Marshall

Rommel's Africa Corps soundly defeated the Americans and British. Even though Ralph and most of his Division did not take part in this battle, they were still alarmed by the defeat. "We thought we would go over there and take care of the Germans quickly."

Not long after the defeat at Kasserine Pass, there was a change in the American command. A new leader emerged on the scene, General George Patton, who became a legend not only for his brilliant battlefield tactics but also for his flamboyant way. "He was as crazy as a bed-bug, but it took guys like that to win the war," Ralph states. "When he arrived, he took one look at us and said we were the sorriest bunch of rag tag soldiers he ever saw." Under Patton's command, American and British forces drove the Nazis out of North Africa by May 1943.

On July 10, 1943, Ralph took part in the Allied invasion of Sicily. Unlike the invasion of Normandy a year later, the Germans controlled the air over Sicily. As the Allied invasion force approached the landing point, they were battered with both ground fire from coastal batteries and air attacks from enemy aircraft. Ralph was huddled below deck on an LST for a landing at Gela when the bombardment started. "I said to myself, 'I'm going up top. If we sink, I don't want to drown like a rat.'" When he emerged from below, he saw German aircraft. "They were flying in perfect formation dropping bombs on us." As the formation passed, a bomb landed and detonated just a few feet to the left of Ralph's landing craft. Then a second bomb landed on the right narrowly missing the craft. "I told Sgt. Taylor standing next to me, 'I am so scared I couldn't eat a cracker.'" The sky was filled with aircraft both friend and foe. On one occasion Ralph overheard an anti-aircraft gunner being berated for firing at an aircraft that was a British Spitfire. Minutes later he witnessed the same gunner receiving orders to fire at anything. In the distance Ralph saw an Allied fuel tanker explode into flames and black smoke. Being frightened was something Ralph freely admitted to me. "If anyone ever tells you he wasn't afraid, he's a liar."

Once ashore, Ralph and the others were quickly pinned down on the beach until after dark. As they lay helplessly on the beach, they could hear the constant roar of approaching aircraft. "They were on us all day," Ralph states. Colonel Hurley, Ralph's Company Commander, was killed during the intense shelling. As night fell, the glow from the stricken gas tanker lit the sky and the battle gradually moved inland. While the battle of Sicily hung in the balance, Ralph and his men evacuated the wounded to makeshift aid stations.

Patton led the 5th Army into Palermo on July 22. Messina fell to the Allies a month later. Nazi defenders were either captured or retreated from Italy. While stationed outside Palermo, many of the men in his unit spoke Italian and would converse with the Sicilians. "We had a lot of guys that could speak Italian. I couldn't understand them people," Ralph says with a chuckle.

Sicily was, at the moment, under Allied control. The Mediterranean was now less hazardous to Allied ships. Sicily would also be used as a staging area for the upcoming Italian campaign. The capture, however, came with a high price tag. Not only was Colonel Hurley killed but Sgt. Fink was also. "He was a great guy. He had a lot of guts; he was a real leader," Ralph recalls about his friend. Losing his close friend was one of Ralph's most difficult times. As we talked, Ralph thumbed through dozens of photos taken by Fink. It was a sobering experience for me to gaze at images captured through the eyes of a man whose life was sacrificed so many years ago.

"Hell on Wheels" was called on again a year later. The operation was larger this time than that of Sicily or North Africa: it was the liberation of France. On June 6, 1944, soldiers of the Allied Expeditionary Force landed on the beaches of Normandy boldly fighting their way on shore. Once a foothold was established, armored divisions were brought in to lead the attack on land.

Before the campaign started, Ralph was promoted to First Sergeant thus giving him the responsibility of setting up mobile aid stations just behind the front lines and commanding the combat medics. "I would send two medics with each company." During the fighting, the medics carried the wounded to the nearest aid station where they were treated before being evacuated to a hospital.

Ralph boarded an LST on June 9 to cross the English Channel. As Ralph stood on the port side of the landing craft, a fellow soldier took his picture that Ralph showed me. In this wrinkled, 2" x 3" black and white photo, the profile of a young soldier's face gazing out onto the water is remarkably captured. The young man was admittedly apprehensive, yet ahead he charged. The photo reveals Ralph as he looked on that day he gallantly joined fellow combat forces to rescue a continent.

Once the landing craft hit Omaha Beach, the gates were opened, and Ralph drove his vehicle onto the beach. Unlike those that had come before him, he entered France unopposed. Ralph saw the signs of the terrible battle that had preceded him by three days. "I looked out and saw helmets floating in the water."

Days later Ralph and other members of the 17th Engineers moved into an area known as the "Norman hedgerows." The Germans had been pushed from the coast by the end of June. However, the hedgerows now stymied the Allied forces. The Germans had managed to bring reinforcements into the area. No longer were the Allies facing units partially made up of older men and young children.

The hedgerows were vast areas of crisscrossing roads surrounded by trees and mounds of dirt. The trees and vegetation were so dense at some points they created walls that tanks could not penetrate. American forces moving into the area soon found themselves in a maze. Visibility was limited at best to a few hundred feet. The Germans were dug in and determined to stop the liberation of France. American tanks crossing through the maze were hit by German artillery and tank fire. The same fate awaited American infantry.

Advance through the hedgerows was painfully slow. In July the 2nd Armored devised a plan of how to cut through the hedgerows by mounting a set of steel bars on the front of the

Sherman tanks. This simple idea allowed the tanks to punch holes in the hedgerows and take the fight to the dug-in Germans.

After successfully fighting through the hedgerows, the advance again stalled near St. Lo where a stalemate occurred between the two armies. On July 21 three thousand Allied bombers attempted to force a retreat by pounding the Germans. Ralph was nearby and witnessed the events. "I told my Captain, 'I think they are dropping their bombs too close to our lines.'" Ralph was right. Miscommunication caused the deaths of hundreds of Americans in that operation. "Later that night, we moved out. As soon as we were in the open, we could hear aircraft. It was German planes dropping bombs on us." Many members of Ralph's unit were caught in the open. Ralph hurried to the rear and obtained a two and a half-ton truck to drive back to the casualty area. Ralph turned on the headlights even though it made him a target. "They were yelling at me to turn those damn lights out. I said, 'I don't care. I have wounded men to pick up.'" He soon had the truck filled with wounded GIs and evacuated them to a treatment area.

By the end of July, the Americans broke out of Normandy via St. Lo. "Once we were through St. Lo, the terrain was flat. That was good tank country," Ralph recalls. The 2nd Armored Division gave chase to the retreating Germans. The British and American Armies encircled the retreating Germans at the Falaise Gap. Ralph recalls one night in August with Capt. Arthur Mark, the Regimental dentist. "We got turned around and were lost. We then found ourselves with the 82nd Reconnaissance. They were our forward unit. I knew we were in trouble; we were up near the front with the big boys." Ralph recalls with a chuckle that after a heated discussion about being lost, "I finally told him, 'if you can do any better, you come over here and drive.'" The pair found their way back at four in the morning. Ralph was tired when he started to dig his foxhole. "I started digging and found I was digging in rock. I just threw the shovel aside and decided to sleep above ground. I thought 'if they get me, they get me.'" After nearly three years of combat, Ralph came to a sobering realization. "I thought to myself, 'I'm probably not going home.'" He was weary and thoughts of a future no longer existed.

After the Falaise Gap, the 17th bypassed Paris and moved to Germany and then to Belgium where Ralph was assigned to Combat Command B. At one point while traveling along a roadway, Ralph looked out and saw another road. "I could see several vehicles passing us in the opposite direction. When I looked closer, I could see they were German." Combat Command A was traveling on a roadway running parallel to and north of the German column. "All at once, we opened up on the Germans. They were caught between us in a crossfire." As Ralph moved forward, he saw that 265 German vehicles had been destroyed. Ralph stopped when he heard the cries of a wounded German. "He was lying in the back of a truck full of dead soldiers. He was asking us for water." Despite the fact he was the enemy, Ralph was haunted by the event.

After Germany surrendered in June, Ralph boarded a liberty ship back to the States. "I had worn the same uniform the entire time I was in Europe. I had enough."

Ralph shared with me the feelings of impending doom he had during his marathon years of service. He commented, "After all that time over there I just accepted that I'm probably going to be killed. I suppose there is a reason I made it back." He then made a statement I have heard from almost every veteran: "I wouldn't take anything for that experience, but I wouldn't do it again for a million dollars."

On the final interview with Ralph for this story, he stated, "Jerry, don't talk about me like I was a hero. I wasn't." I replied, "Sure you weren't, Ralph. Sure you weren't." Ralph is simply a man who loved his country so much he volunteered for service. While doing so he was told to go overseas for three years. He slept in the sand of Africa … beneath the stars of Sicily … in the mud of France. He was a warrior yet he helped save lives, both American and German. Everything that was asked of him he did. Isn't that what a hero does?

It was an honor to serve
God Bless America
Ray E Sills

RAY SELLS

FRIDAY THE 13TH

Ray Sells was born on July 1, 1924, in the town of Twinton, Tennessee. Just four months after his birth, his father passed away. Ray and his two siblings weren't left fatherless for long ...his uncle, Roy Winningham, stepped in to help provide for the kids.

Uncle Roy worked at a local coal mine until a violent strike forced him to leave Twinton to look for work. Jobs were scarce in the area, so Roy's search led him to McDonald, Ohio. He found employment in the steel mill and soon after sent for Ray's family.

Growing up in a steel mill town was pretty average for Ray. "Everybody knew everyone else." Ray attended McDonald High School. His older brother, Harold, joined the Navy after he graduated and was stationed on board the battleship U.S.S. Maryland. Life in 1941 was as predictable as it gets for a young man living in the Midwest. Ray was a senior at McDonald High. Then news broke on December 7, 1941, that Pearl Harbor had been attacked. The entire nation was in shock. Events of that fateful morning were even more troubling for Ray's family knowing the U.S.S. Maryland was at Pearl Harbor. Several anxious days later, word came from Harold ...he was slightly wounded but ok. "He was fortunate he came out of it alright," Ray says about his big brother.

In the spring of 1943, Ray was drafted into the U.S. Army. He was 18 on May 1 when he left for basic training at Camp Shelby. He learned the basics of marching and firing an M1 rifle with other men from Ohio like Herman Milano, Tom Snowden, and Eddie Stiner. The quiet life in McDonald was no more. What awaited Ray was two years of shear deprivation. What would be required of him was two years of raw courage.

November 3, 1943, Ray boarded a troop ship for an 18-day voyage across the Atlantic to Casablanca, North Africa. The stay in Casablanca was brief. On Christmas day, Ray boarded another ship and made the journey through the Mediterranean Sea to Naples, Italy, where Ray was absorbed into the 36th Infantry Division, "The Texans." Ray served as a private first class with Company A of the 141st Regiment.

Italy at that time was aligned with Germany and Japan to form the Axis powers. Soon after Allied forces landed in Sicily and Italy, an armistice was agreed upon between the Italian government and the Allies. Italy was no longer at war yet the German army remained in Italy. The Allied forces now faced the unenviable task of routing out the German army occupying the mountains and valleys of Italy. The fighting was tough; the terrain favored the Germans.

One of the most frightening nights Ray had in combat was one of his first. "I was assigned guard duty. There I was in the middle of the night standing on a mountain in Italy. I was only 19 years old, all alone and scared to death."

Near the town of Cassino, the fighting had come to a stalemate. The Germans had set up defensive positions intent to hold the Allied advance in an area known as the "Gustav line." During the struggle, the Nazis held the high ground. An ancient Benedictine Monastery was perched atop the mountain overlooking Cassino. The age-old building was breathtaking in its grandeur. Unfortunately war heeds little admiration for beauty or heritage. Even things esteemed or holy can be utilized for dominance. The Germans occupied the monastery, which provided a perfect observation point to see American movement below. German artillery and machine gun positions fired down on any attempt to capture the high ground. It seemed as if the monastery alone was stopping the advance.

Beneath the monastery ran the Rapido River. The Rapido was only 45 to 50 feet wide yet its current was mighty. It was a dividing line between the two armies. The Germans held the west. In January Ray and his Regiment were sent to fight their way across the river near the town of Sant` Angelo to outflank the Germans holding the monastery.

Ray's company gathered in a wooded area near the river. The engineers had located a minefield near the banks of the river and feverously worked to locate the mines before the foot soldiers attempted to cross. "They used white pieces of tape and surgical gauze to show the mines they located." In some cases the wind and concussion of artillery blew the markers away from the mines. "We still had men step on the mines as we attempted to cross the field," Ray recalls.

Company A, under continuous attack from machine guns and artillery, reached the riverbank. Then boats were brought forward. The date was January 20; PFC Ray Sells was merely a boy serving in his first combat. Ray and other members of Company A should have been back home in school or working. Yet here they were, preparing to cross a foreign river, in what would be one of the boldest actions of the Italian Campaign.

After nightfall several attempts were made to cross the river in boats, but the current was too strong. Some of the boats were useless when hit by even the smallest amount of enemy fire. A strategy was formulated for the combat engineers to construct a bridge across the river. Shortly after midnight, the bridge was in place. The river crossing was attempted at 2 am. Ray recalls the order. "'Company A, let's go,' is what I heard. I fell into line and we started across." Ray was part of the first group to cross. "I may have been the fifth or sixth man in line." Darkness was their only cover against enemy fire as they hurried across. Within seconds Ray made it to the west bank of the Rapido. Just a handful of men were ahead of him and about three dozen followed. Abruptly German gunfire found the bridge. "Only a few of us made it across when the bridge was hit." Ray's group was now cut off from the rest of the Regiment. As the unyielding enemy fire came in, some of the men attempted a retreat back across the river. "I saw some of the guys try to swim back. The current was very strong and the water was cold. It was January," Ray recalls.

Now on the western side of the objective, the remnants of Company A moved inward away from the river. The crack of small arms fire continued. Grass and a few trees provided the only cover. "Once we made our way away from the river, we hit the ground." They remained on the ground until sunrise. It was thought that more troops would soon follow the few that initially crossed at 0200 hours. As it became light, the reinforcements were yet to join. "We had been ordered to go across a couple hundred yards and stay put, so that's what we did. Our officers were real green and so were most of us. I didn't even know the names of our officers." Ray was joined by no less than twelve men he had trained with at Camp Shelby. Among them were Snowden, Stiner, Milano and Mike Santora of West Virginia. Of the men who had trained with Ray in the States, they had a combined total of four hours combat experience. Everything was quiet as the sun rose. "All at once we heard a machine gun firing at us from a farmhouse ahead." Tom Snowden was able to move in close enough to lob a grenade into the upstairs window. "He was always a wild man," Ray says about Snowden with a smile. "We think he knocked the gun out." Again silence fell around Company A. One of the men near Ray, Sgt. Murphy, had been wounded in the shoulder. "That was the first time I had met the guy. I put my coat over him, and we carried him off."

By mid-morning, Ray and the others were still alone in enemy territory. They had other problems too …they had only the ammo and food carried with them. Inexperience would now cause a major blunder for the group. "We didn't hear or see anything. We took our packs off, and I stopped to smoke." The group was in the open with no cover when shots rang out. "All hell broke loose. We were being fired at from every direction. All I could do was lay face down in the grass." Ray was lying next to Mike Santora. The group of forty or so men had no cover from the incoming enemy fire. Most of them lay motionless on the ground. Some made a futile attempt to return fire. As time passed, the enemy fire intensified as it moved closer. "I heard the second lieutenant give the order to cease fire." After a few moments, the fire stopped. Ray could see German soldiers approaching. The men around him slowly rose to their feet and placed their hands above their heads. Ray did the same. As he glanced around, Ray saw several of his comrades still motionless on the ground. The enemy fire had hit them. Some of the men lying there had also trained with Ray back in the States. This too had been their first time in combat.

Ray Sells and the others were now prisoners of war. The date was January 22, 1944. "The first thing they did was search us. They then took us to a house, and we were interrogated. We were only required to give our name, rank and serial number. I was only a private first class. They knew I didn't know anything." Within a day, they were loaded on a train ... crammed inside with other POWs in total darkness. The train took them north through Italy. "I think we were in that boxcar for three days. They had placed a barrel with straw in it for us to use as a toilet. None of us ever used it. We hadn't had anything to eat or drink and didn't need it." Their first stop was Stalag IV B in Muhlburg, Poland. Then they were moved to Stalag II B in Hammerstein. After a week, Ray was transferred to a camp at Felstow near the Baltic Sea. The date was February 18, 1944. Ray was still wearing his government issued uniform, which now bore a red triangle painted on his pants and coat. Not long after arriving, Ray was assigned to fieldwork detail in a group of twelve men. Their work consisted of cleaning horse stalls, building fences and chopping wood. "We were required to chop three cubic yards a day. That's a lot of wood." Ray didn't mind the work. "Being in the work group had its advantages. If you stayed in the Stalag, you were only able to eat what was rationed. We were able to gather as many potatoes and beets as we wanted." Stiner, Santora and Milano were also with Ray at the camp.

Security was surprisingly light at the camp. One or two guards supervised the work crew. Escape would have done little good for Ray and the others due to their proximity to the

Russian front. It was impossible to reach the American lines from the Baltic. At times a civilian farmer, a middle-aged man from the village, would oversee their work. "He would sit around and tell us about his family," Ray recalls.

Back in Ohio, Ray's mother Trissie hadn't heard about Ray's capture until a letter written by Ray came from the American Red Cross. Ray told his mother that he was a prisoner of war. The letter went on to say that he was all right and being treated well. "When I wrote that letter, I was hungry and scared to death; but I didn't want her to worry." A few weeks later, a representative of the Defense Department knocked on her door. He told Mrs. Sells that Ray was missing in action. Then Ray's mother showed him Ray's letter. "Mom said you should have seen the look on his face."

They remained on the farm through fall with little word of the Allied advance after D-Day. In all, Ray states they were treated well at the work camp in Felstow. "I can't say we were mistreated by the guards." They remained there through the winter of 1944 and into the new year. By now the Russians were descending on the Baltic Sea.

On February 18, 1945, the POWs had been held at Felstow for a year. They were ordered to gather their belongings and all the food they could carry to move to another Stalag. On that day Ray along with about 100 POWs and 12 German guards headed east. "As we marched, the Russian artillery could be heard in the distance." Some men were forced to discard some of the food early in the march. The weight of the rations was too heavy. At night they slept in barns or any other shelter they could find. On March 5, they stopped at Swinemünde Bay. "I remember sleeping on the ground that night under the stars. It was my grandmother's birthday." Two weeks into the forced march, the food ran out. Not only were the POWs hungry, so were the guards. As the days passed, both guards and POWs began to disappear from the group. Ray isn't sure what happened. "I think that maybe small groups of POWs and guards just walked off during the night."

By the end of March, there was little to keep the POWs from simply leaving. There was surely nothing preventing the guards themselves from deserting and most did. Ray and his buddies from Camp Shelby agreed to stay together. There was no longer a destination for the wandering men. They would move in different directions from day to day ... east one day, maybe west the next. After more than a month of wandering, both the Americans and Germans were as one. As they set out each day, they had but one common objective--find food. The German guard that had supervised Ray at the work farm still remained with the group. "He was about 30. He had always treated me fair at the camp," Ray states.

During the first week of April, the group stopped at a German airbase for the night. During the night, Ray could no longer bear his hunger. He left the barracks they had been told to stay in and walked to the building the guards were using. As Ray approached the door, he saw the Germans playing cards. Ray motioned to the guard from his work camp. "He was playing cards with the others and stopped. He walked over to me. I told him I was hungry. He walked away and in a few minutes came back. He passed me a piece of bread without the other guards seeing him." Even though this man had supervised Ray for over a year, Ray never knew his name. "He was brave for giving me that food. He could have gotten in a lot of trouble for that." While at the air base, the group faced their most dangerous time. During the night, American aircraft bombed the base. Fortunately, Ray and the others were uninjured.

On Friday, April 13, PFC Ray Sells had been a prisoner of war for 448 days and had been on the move the last 55 days. The original group had dwindled to twelve men and two guards. At one point, Ray had eaten a piece of bread with bacon grease on it that gave him dysentery. He was only 20 yet he felt like an old man. While marching the group saw an American artillery spotter flying overhead. Amazingly the two German guards did not interfere when the men started motioning to the aircraft. The small plane circled and landed in a nearby field. "We told the pilot we were prisoners. He said he was going to radio in our position, and then took off."

The men saw a farmhouse a few hundred feet away near the highway. When the group went to the door, an older German woman greeted them, retreated into her home, and returned with a large platter of food. Unfortunately, two soldiers of the elite German SchutzStaffel (SS) arrived at the same time. The woman panicked when she saw the SS and ran back into the house. The pair ordered the men back onto the roadway and told them the direction in which to march. The SS then mounted their motorcycles and proceeded east.

After enduring 55 days of hunger and the elements together, an unexpected alliance formed between the German guards and the American prisoners. One of the most amazing events I have heard about World War II happened when one of the guards pulled the pistol from his holster and handed it to one of the Americans. The guard said, "If the SS return, shoot them." The group then made its way back to the roadway. "All of the sudden, we heard the roar of engines behind us," Ray recalls. About 100 yards away were elements of the American 5th Armored Division. Their rescue was now in site. Without speaking the group started running. Ray was so weak, he fell behind. "I was only 20 years old, but I was bringing up the rear."

Ray and the other POWs told the Unit's commanding officer about the two German guards who were now themselves POWs. "These guys are alright. They treated us good," Ray told him. Ray never saw the guard who had helped him after that day, nor does he know his fate.

"The first thing we ate were pancakes with sugar sprinkled on them. They just put them in our hands. We didn't mind. It was food." Ray was kept in a house that night. In spite of his exhaustion, Ray was too excited to sleep during his first night of freedom. "I have considered Friday the 13th a lucky day every since."

After hearing Ray's story, the time came to ask him his definition of a hero. Although his actions crossing the Rapido

River are as gallant as any written about in this book, Ray stated, "I'm not sure what a hero is, but I'm not one." Ray then said, "I'm just a guy who sacrificed 448 days of his life." I then asked, "What did you sacrifice them for?" "America and freedom" was his simple response.

In his own mind, Ray Sells isn't a hero. To all Americans who enjoy the freedom he sacrificed those 448 days for, he is.

(Tom McFeely is second from the right)

TOM McFEELY

MY UNCLE

While writing this book, I stood atop my soapbox preaching to World War II veterans that they should share their stories with their families. I have talked with family members who know few details of their deceased loved one's war service record. I have done research for families of veterans who have asked for my help. All the while, I have acted like a Saturday night evangelist preaching the sins of losing an important part of our collective history. You can probably guess what happened along the way ...the preacher was a hypocrite.

In 1920 my mother, Mildred Jent, was born into extreme poverty in Kentucky. While very young, she and her two sisters, Meredith and Margerette, moved to a part of Indianapolis called "the valley." When my Aunt Meredith (better known as Reedie) attended high school, she met a 15-year old named Tom McFeely. The two of them became steadies and stayed that way for sixty years.

My fondest memory of Uncle Tom is that he has always been with me on my birthday. You see, Aunt Reedie started a tradition at my birth; she never missed seeing me on my birthday. She always said she would stop the tradition when I married, but old habits are hard to break. We still celebrated at my mother's home for years after my wedding. Uncle Tom always stayed informed of my meteoric high school athletic career. He even lent me his prize putter when I spent a summer chasing that white ball. A man of few words, he is always pleasant and willing to laugh at a joke, loves to fish, and lives to golf.

It has been common family knowledge that my Aunts Reedie and Margerette joined the Navy during the war serving in the WAVES. Over the years Uncle Tom's service record, however, has been a mystery. "Uncle Tom was in the Navy; no I think he was in the Army stationed in England." No one I asked seemed to know for sure.

One morning I called my mother, and Uncle Tom answered the phone. While catching up with each other, I mentioned the book. "What's it about?" he asked. Jokingly I said, "It's about something that happened after you were born, World War II." Uncle Tom stated, "I know a little about it ...I was in it." I then asked, "What exactly did you do during the war?" "I served all the way across France with the 3rd Armored Division," was his reply. I nearly dropped the phone. The 3rd Armored Division was one of the most storied divisions of the war with a combat record of legendary proportions. "The Spearhead," they were called.

As soon as I heard of his service record, I knew my uncle would have to sit down and talk with me. He finally agreed, but other family members were present causing the experience to be even more uncomfortable for Uncle Tom. My nephew and I focused on his every word. I could tell it was difficult for my uncle to tell his story, not because of a long ago traumatic experience, but because he wasn't about to brag to his own family about his adventures.

Uncle Tom was a sergeant with the 451st Engineer Regiment, 3rd Armored Division. He landed at Normandy, France, in the summer of 1944. His regiment was responsible for building and replacing bridges throughout France. During the campaign against the Germans, American tanks couldn't advance without bridges. His job was crucial to the war effort.

Uncle Tom wasn't a by-the-book sergeant. On more than one occasion, he was called on the carpet for allowing his subordinates to call him "Mac." In George Patton's spit and polish 3rd Army, such a breach of military conduct was unthinkable.

When the Germans counterattacked in the Ardennes, Uncle Tom's regiment was rushed to the front. Even though they were bridge builders, they were soldiers first. Bulldozers and hammers were replaced with M-1 rifles and hand grenades.

While advancing through waist-high snow, my uncle's squad encountered the enemy on numerous occasions. They fought with some and captured others. Nightfall brought below zero temperatures. Daylight brought German artillery. "We would dig in and hold our positions. When the artillery came in on us, the shrapnel would cut through the trees," Uncle Tom recalled.

The Spearhead fought across France, Belgium and into Germany. In August of 1945, Uncle Tom returned to Indianapolis on a troop train. He was to have a brief furlough and then be re-deployed to the Pacific Theater of operations. Just as the train arrived at Union Station, the men were met with a strange sight. "People were jumping around and celebrating when we pulled in. It had just been announced the Japanese had surrendered."

The war was over for Uncle Tom and Aunt Reedie. They soon returned to civilian life. My aunt refused to drive but liked to stay on the go. This wasn't a problem for Uncle Tom. It just meant he had to keep plenty of gas in the car and always be ready to drive when Aunt Reedie gave the marching orders. My aunt lived a happy life after the war mainly because the man she had chosen to be her husband was a good man who was always good to her.

Their wartime experience was something they were both quiet about. In 1999 my Aunt Reedie passed away. Her coffin was draped with the Stars and Stripes. Three representatives of the United States Navy were present at her graveside service. I'm sure some of the people present wondered why they were there. Some of us wondered how the Navy was notified. We later learned that Uncle Tom had quietly made the arrangements. We were glad he did. After all, it was a privilege both of them had earned more than 50 years ago.

After I finished firing questions at my Uncle Tom, he had but one thing to say. "When you write about me, just say I went over there and was lucky enough to come home."

My uncle is yet another example of the quiet dignity that envelops the men and women who fought and won World War II. I'm sure he rarely looks back at what he once did or realizes its importance. Nevertheless, the pride will be all mine whenever I announce that my uncle once fought with the 3rd Armored Division.

CLOSING

I have heard two statements from almost every person in this book. I agree with them both. "I wouldn't take a million dollars for the experience but I wouldn't want to do it again," most have said. What they accomplished wasn't easy yet they are glad they did it. Another common statement was, "I'm not anyone special." This too may be correct. Millions of other men and woman that served during World War Two are still with us. I'm confident you may know some. I urge you to hear their story. Take the time to know just how much they have done for you.

None of them would ever ask for recognition or appreciation for what they did. I suggest you thank them in your own way. Whenever you vote or go to church, thank them. Whenever you speak your mind or gather for dinner, thank them. When you tuck your children or grandchildren into a safe bed tonight, you should thank them. To all the Heroes of the Heartland, thank you.

"Every one who was over there was a hero."
         Alton Pugh
         77th Infantry Division